BEGINNERACOUSTIC
FINGERSTYLEGUITAR

The Complete Guide to Playing Fingerstyle Acoustic Guitar

SIMON**PRATT**

FUNDAMENTAL**CHANGES**

Beginner Acoustic Fingerstyle Guitar

The Complete Guide to Playing Fingerstyle Acoustic Guitar

ISBN: 978-1-78933-178-3

Published by **www.fundamental-changes.com**

www.fundamental-changes.com

Over 11,000 fans on Facebook: **FundamentalChangesInGuitar**

Instagram: **FundamentalChanges**

For over 350 Free Guitar Lessons with Videos Check Out

www.fundamental-changes.com

Cover Image is Taylor Builder's Edition 324ce. Copyright Taylor Guitars, used by permission.

Contents

Introduction

When I look back over my guitar career, one of my happiest memories is learning to fingerpick. Although it wasn't an easy process, it has been one of the most rewarding things I've ever done. To be given the chance to write a book about it now by Fundamental Changes is truly an honour. In this book, I want to help you avoid the pitfalls and traps that I fell into when learning to fingerpick, and provide you with a concise, structured method to learn to play fingerstyle guitar.

This book is aimed at guitarists who are learning to fingerpick for the first time, so it builds layer-on-layer, focusing closely on each step of the process before moving on. You may have picked up this book because you're a fan of acoustic music, have recently picked up the guitar, and you want to learn to fingerpick the right way from the beginning. Or you might be an experienced guitarist who has never gotten around to learning to fingerpick properly. This book is for you too! Fingerpicking is the nemesis of many a highly experienced player. While it's possible to get by as a musician with occasional mediocre fingerpicking, it is so much more rewarding to be able to do it right! It's never too late to perfect an area of technique on guitar and this book will teach you the right way to go about it.

We will begin with the absolute basics of which finger should pluck which string and master the mechanics of fingerpicking. By the end of this book you'll be able to attempt a specially written performance piece. Here, I've endeavoured to write something that will push you a little bit, but not so much that you won't want to attempt it.

If you are new to this style, I recommend working through the book from start to finish. Take your time to work through each section. Make sure you feel comfortable with the material in each chapter before you move on. It's not a race, so make sure you just enjoy making music.

The exercises in this book will work equally well on an acoustic or electric guitar, but the audio examples were recorded on a Taylor acoustic guitar.

The audio for this book is available from **http://www.fundamental-changes.com/download-audio**

I highly recommend you go and download it now, as it will help you to hear exactly how each example should be played.

Finally, before we get started, I want to recommend a list of my favourite fingerstyle pieces. I suggest that you take some time to draw inspiration from these before you dive into the first chapter.

James Taylor – *Fire and Rain*

Dire Straits – *Romeo And Juliet*

Extreme – *More Than Words*

Jack Johnson – *Belle*

Mason Williams – *Classical Gas*

Tommy Emmanuel – *Angelina / Mombasa*

Kansas – *Dust in The Wind*

Led Zeppelin – *Babe I'm Gonna Leave You*

Fleetwood Mac – *Landslide*

Red Hot Chili Peppers – *Scar Tissue*

Simon And Garfunkel – *The Boxer*

Ralph McTell – *Streets of London*

Happy Playing!

Simon

Get the Audio

The audio files for this book are available to download for free from **www.fundamental-changes.com.** The link is in the top right-hand corner. Simply select this book title from the drop-down menu and follow the instructions to get the audio.

We recommend that you download the files directly to your computer, not to your tablet, and extract them there before adding them to your media library. You can then put them on your tablet, iPod or burn them to CD. On the download page there is a help PDF and we also provide technical support via the contact form.

Over 11,000 fans on Facebook: FundamentalChangesInGuitar

Tag us for a share on Instagram:

@FundamentalChanges

@simeygoesfunky

For over 350 Free Guitar Lessons with Videos Check Out

www.fundamental-changes.com

Get the Video

To help you master the longer pieces in this book, we have included performance videos that you can watch online. To access them, simply navigate to

www.fundamental-changes.com/beginner-acoustic-videos

Watch them before you learn the pieces, and make sure you download the audio from the previous page. It'll make your journey a lot more fun, musical and productive!

Chapter One – The Mechanics of Great Fingerstyle Technique

"Fingerstyle guitar technique" simply means to use your fingers and thumb to pluck the strings, rather than a pick. Perfecting this technique relies on learning to coordinate your picking hand fingers and training them to pick the correct strings in sequence.

The thumb and fingers are assigned to specific strings and named using the acronym PIMA. This is inherited from Classical guitar technique, so the names are in Spanish:

p = pulgar (thumb)

i = indice (index finger)

m = medio (middle finger)

a = anular (ring finger)

Whenever you see a musical example in this book, there will be a letter written alongside each note to tell you which finger (or your thumb) should be used to play the note. You'll notice that the pinky finger has been left out. This is because the pinky is not normally used in fingerstyle. If it does crop up in a piece of music, it will usually be labelled "c". (The diagram below illustrates a right-handed player. If you are left-handed, everything is reversed).

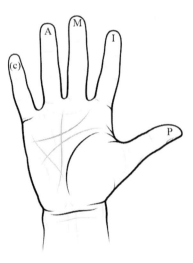

- The thumb (p) will normally play the three lowest strings on the guitar (E, A and D strings)

- The index finger (i) will play the G string

- The middle finger (m) will play the B string

- and the ring finger (a) will play the high E string

Getting the correct position

It's important to get the picking hand arm, wrist and fingers into the correct position to play. Beginner players often make life difficult for themselves in this regard, simply through bad positioning. The aim is to have a well-balanced, relaxed position, so that the fingers are placed to pluck the strings easily. Having the right position makes it much easier to ensure each finger strikes its assigned string cleanly. Look at the picture below and follow these three simple rules:

1. Rest your forearm just below the elbow on the lower bout of the guitar body

2. Allow your wrist to curve slightly, so you can touch the strings with your fingers

3. Avoid anchoring your hand or fingers on the guitar body

If you're in any doubt over whether you've got the position right, ask yourself, *are my arm and wrist relaxed? Am I straining to pluck the strings?* Make small adjustments until you feel relaxed and comfortable.

A word about chord diagrams

Throughout this book, you'll see chords presented as diagrams. The following images show how the written notation of a chord diagram translates to where you place your fingers on the neck. Pay careful attention to which strings are played and which fingers are used. Open strings are indicated by an "O" symbol and strings that should be muted by an "X".

The diagram below shows the notes on each of the open strings of the guitar. The second diagram shows you how to number the fingers of the fretting hand. The third diagram shows the standard way chords are notated on chord *grids*. Each dot represents where you place a finger. The final diagram shows how the notation relates to where you place your fingers on the guitar neck.

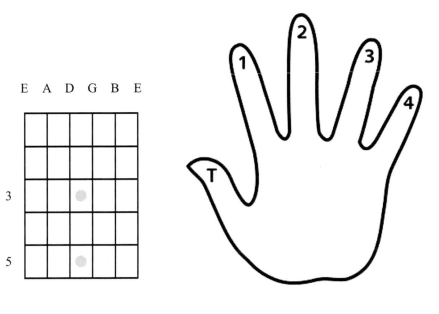

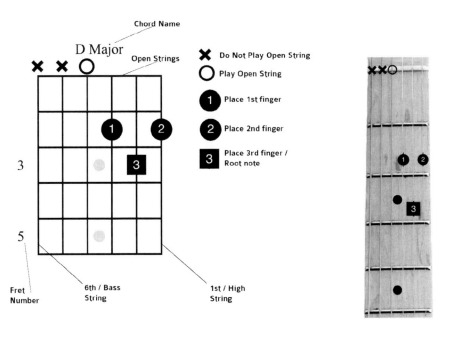

First Exercises

We're going to dive into some foundational exercises to get you started. Some of these early exercises may seem very basic – especially if you've been playing a while but are new to fingerstyle – but the aim is to build a solid foundation for your fingerstyle technique. I want to help you reach the point where the technique becomes automatic and you don't even have to think about it. Don't be tempted to rush! If you spend some time perfecting these techniques, in the future you'll be able to play with great accuracy and consistency.

In order to train your fingers, we'll start with the thumb, then add one finger at a time. Use a metronome for these exercises (there are plenty of free apps to download to your phone or tablet).

Listen to the audio for these examples and you'll hear that mostly I allow the notes to ring into each other. You can practice these examples with a "let ring" feel and without.

In Example 1a, pluck the low E string with your thumb (*p*) four times, one for each click of an 80 beats per minute (bpm) metronome. As you pluck the open string with your thumb, make sure that you are not accidentally hitting any other open strings in the process. Aim to make each note the same volume.

Example 1a

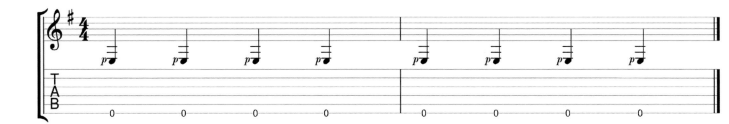

Now hold down this simple open E minor chord:

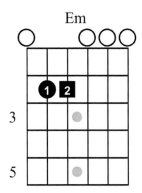

We will be using this chord shape for the majority of examples in this chapter.

To play Example 1b, hold down the E minor chord above. With your thumb, pluck the low E, A and D strings, then the A string again, playing one note per beat. Repeat this exercise several times until you can sound each note smoothly and with a consistent volume. Listen to the audio example before you play. This exercise is designed for you to "loop" around, over and over. We'll quickly move on to more exciting stuff, but it's important to train your thumb, so play this lots of times.

Example 1b

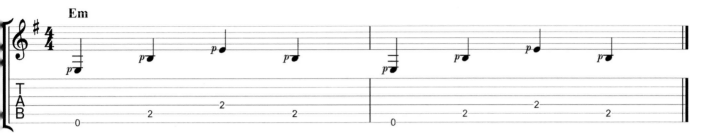

Once you feel comfortable using your thumb to fingerpick different strings you can add in your index finger to pluck the E minor chord shape. The index finger will *always* be used to pluck the G string. In Example 1c, use your thumb to play the first three notes of the chord and your index finger to play the open G string.

For some reason, lots of people are tempted to pluck the D string with their index finger on the way back down, but don't do this! Descend back down the strings using the *thumb*. It's important to keep your thumb and fingers assigned to their designated strings. Once again, play this exercise lots of times to get it sounding smooth and even.

Example 1c

Now we will play the E minor chord shape again and this time add in the middle finger to pluck the B string.

Example 1d

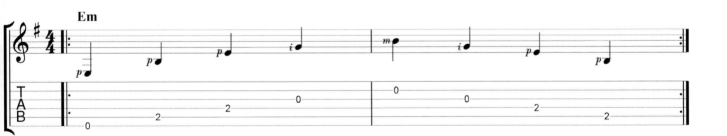

Finally, in order to fingerpick the E minor chord across all six strings, we need to introduce the ring finger to play the note on the high E string. This is demonstrated in Example 1e.

As uninspiring as it may sound, you should dedicate plenty of time to practising just Example 1e. This is the most common and fundamental ascending/descending fingerstyle picking pattern. If you nail this, then you will sound good, whatever chord you happen to be playing.

It's crucial at this stage to work at it until you can execute the pattern cleanly, with no fluffed notes, and with a consistent volume between each string. You are training your fingers for the future! In a moment you will do some exercises that will help to work on perfecting this note separation.

Example 1e

Important note! Only move on to the following examples when you feel completely comfortable with the previous exercises. It doesn't matter if it takes a few days or a couple of weeks to master the examples, it just matters that each string sounds clearly when played and that the correct fingers are used to complete the examples.

Separating fingerpicks

When you have mastered the basic ascending/descending picking pattern, it's time to develop your picking hand dexterity by plucking notes that are further apart. Alternating between your thumb and different fingers will help you to achieve this. Keep holding down the open E minor chord for all these examples.

We'll start simple. Example 1f alternates between plucking the open low E string with your thumb and the open G string with your index finger.

Example 1f

Now we'll increase the distance between the strings. Play the low E string with your thumb as before and pluck the B string with your middle finger. When you've been used to playing adjacent strings, it's tempting to think, "Yes, I've got this!" but skipping strings demands much greater accuracy and control. As before, it's important to go slowly and to develop this accuracy over time.

Example 1g

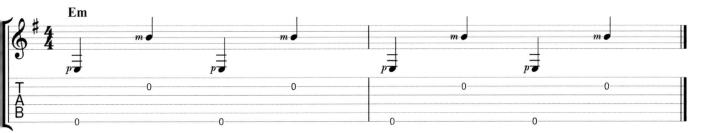

Now pluck the low E with your thumb and high E with your ring finger.

Example 1h

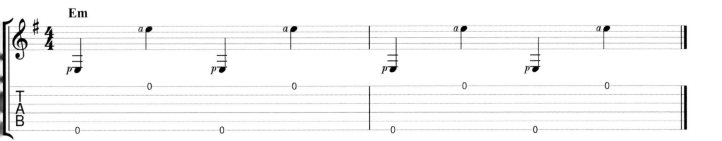

Take some time to practise these patterns. The purpose is to train your fingers to pluck the correct string *every time*. Try playing examples 1f to 1h back to back and keep looping them around. Don't move on to the following exercises until you can consistently target strings with the correct finger.

First Patterns

Now let's explore some commonly used fingerpicking patterns. Example 1i is a popular pattern that combines a low bass note and the three highest strings. You will have heard this pattern used on many records.

Fret the open E minor chord as before and pluck the low E string followed by the G, B and high E strings in sequence. You will use your thumb, index, middle and ring fingers in turn. (This pattern is very similar to *Nothing Else Matters* by Metallica. Have a listen!)

An easy way to remember this pattern is by the string number sequence. Remember, string six is the *thickest* string and string one is the *thinnest*. So, we can refer to this pattern as: **6 3 2 1**. Here's a quick reminder of which fingers are assigned to the strings:

- Play the low E string with your thumb *(p)*

- Play the G string with your index finger *(i)*

- Play the B string with your middle finger *(m)*

- Play the high E string with your ring finger *(a)*

Example 1i

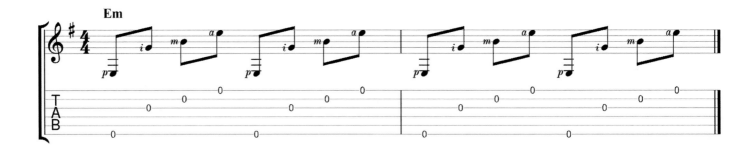

We can reverse the sequence of the top three strings to create another common folk fingerstyle pattern. This pattern is played…

- Thumb (p) on the low E string

- Ring (a) finger on the high E string

- Middle (m) finger on the B string

- Index (i) finger on the G string

This pattern can be expressed as **6 1 2 3**

Example 1j

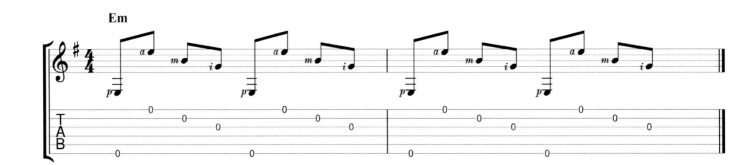

Patterns where each string is played in sequence are easier to get to grips with than ones where the fingers are required to alternate, so we'll work to develop that skill next. Once again holding down our E minor chord, this pattern is played:

- Thumb (p) on the low E string

- Middle (m) finger on the B string

- Index (i) finger on the G string

- Ring (a) finger on the high E string

It may be easier for you to memorise this pattern as **6 2 3 1**.

Example 1k

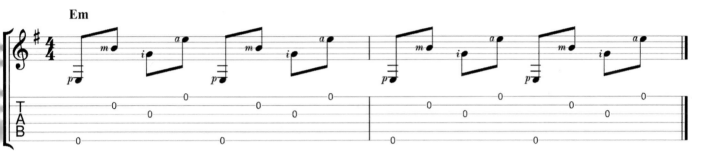

Here is another picking variation. In Example 1l, the picking sequence is:

- Thumb (p) on the low E string

- Ring (a) finger on the high E string

- Index (i) finger on the G string

- Middle (m) finger on the B string

For easy of remembering, think of this pattern as **6 1 3 2**

Example 1l

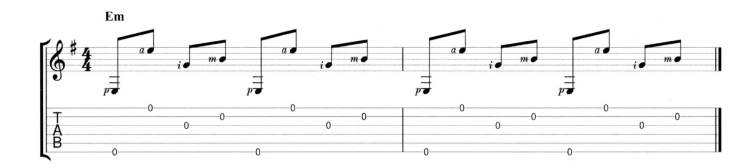

Once again, I'll stress how important it is to give yourself adequate time to learn and internalise each of these four patterns. They will form the bedrock of your picking style for years to come. I suggest working with one pattern at a time and, when you're comfortable, switching between them. Vary the pattern as you continue to hold down a chord.

Two Notes at Once

The next challenge in fingerpicking is to get used to playing more than one string at once. We will develop this technique as we go, but as usual we will start simple. Fret the open E minor chord and pluck the low E and G strings *at the same time* using your thumb and index finger.

Example 1m

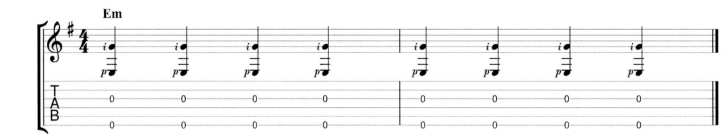

These exercises are all about training your fingers to be in the right place at the right time, so this time pluck the low E and B strings simultaneously with your thumb and middle finger.

Example 1n

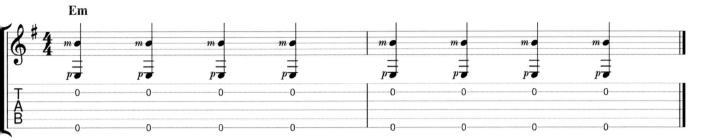

To complete the sequence, play the low and high E strings simultaneously with your thumb and ring finger.

Example 1o

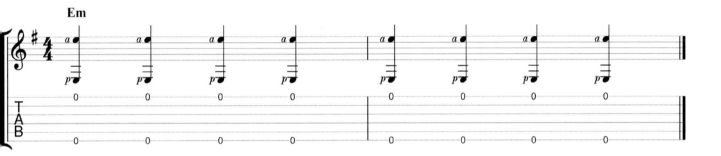

This may seem very simple, but you need ensure the strings sound perfectly in sync, as next we will be changing strings while keeping the bass note going. Take as much time as you need before moving on. The end goal is finger independence, where each finger automatically goes to the right string at the right time.

For Example 1p, keep the low E string going with your thumb, while your index and middle fingers play the open G and B strings respectively.

Example 1p

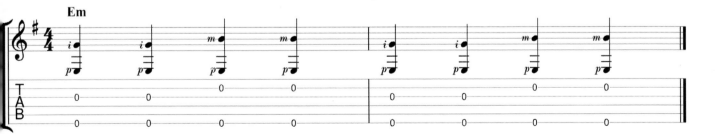

Example 1q is similar, but this time we skip the B string. While your thumb keeps the low E going, play the open G and high E strings with your index and ring fingers respectively.

Example 1q

The final pattern combines the low E bass note with the open B and high E strings, played with the middle and ring fingers.

Example 1r

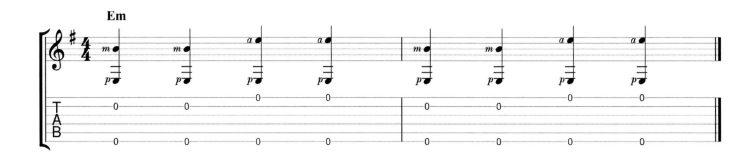

Combining Single Notes and Multiple Notes

Now you're ready to combine single notes and multiple notes and play them in useful patterns. The following patterns use our E minor chord and combine single bass notes with multiple notes on adjacent strings. Listen to the audio to hear how these examples are played.

Example 1s shows a pattern that alternates between the low E string and plucking the G and B strings at the same time. Knowing which fingers to use should be becoming automatic but check the fingering instructions on the notation if you need to.

Example 1s

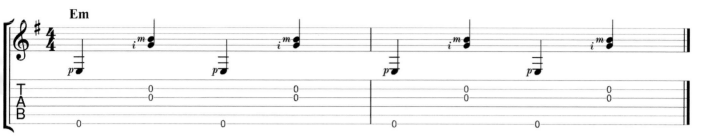

Next practice plucking the low E string followed by the B and high E strings in unison.

Example 1t

Example 1u combines the previous two patterns as a one-bar phrase. While you keep the low E bass note going, alternate between the open G and B strings, and open B and high E strings. Make sure you use the correct finger combinations to pluck the higher string chord fragments. Use a metronome too! It's important to keep the bass note playing in time. It's easy to think you're playing perfectly in time, but often the metronome will disagree!

Example 1u

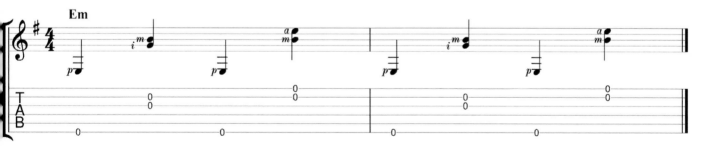

You can, of course, become more creative with your fingerpicking patterns and combine examples from throughout this chapter. For instance, Example 1v uses the **6 3 2 1** pattern to pluck each string individually, then plays the low E string followed by a chord fragment on the G and B strings.

Example 1v

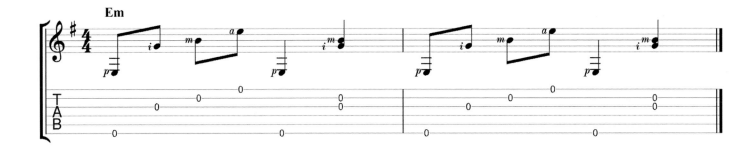

The next example is the same as the previous one, but on the last beat play the chord fragment on the B and high E strings instead.

Example 1w

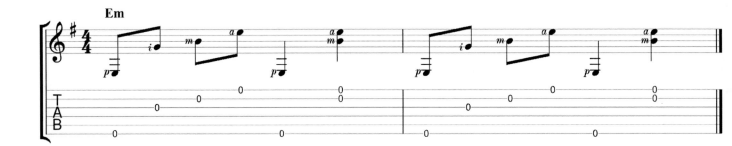

In order to improve as a fingerstyle guitarist, you can gradually build coordination and dexterity in the picking hand by varying the most common patterns. Example 1x uses the **6 1 2 3** pattern then plays the low E string followed by a chord fragment on the G and B strings.

Example 1x

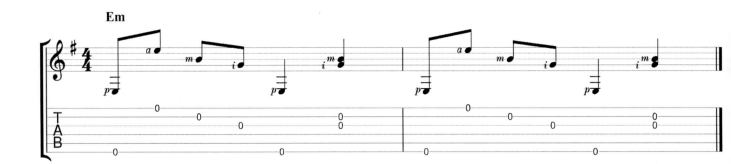

Example 1y is identical to the previous example but this time pluck the B and high E strings together on the last beat.

Example 1y

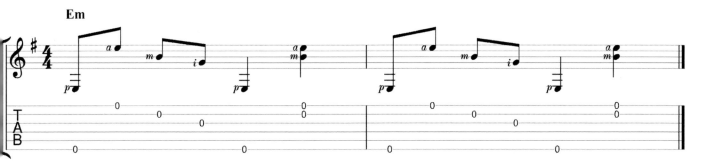

Once you have worked through this chapter in detail, pick your five favourite patterns and write down their example numbers in the chart below. This will act as a quick reference when you want to practice or write your own fingerpicking pieces. In the second box write what you like about this pattern (maybe something like, "flows well under the fingers" or "reminds me of X song". Put a tick in the third column when you've learnt to play the pattern from memory and no longer need the book to play it.

Favourite Patterns	What I like about this pattern is	Can play without reading the book
Example		
Example		
Example		
Example		
Example		

Chapter Two – How to Apply Picking Patterns to Chord Progressions

Now that you've spent time working on the essential fingerpicking patterns, it's time to apply them to chord progressions. It's one thing picking through a single, static chord, but having to play multiple chord shapes while keeping a consistent picking hand pattern will test how well you've learnt the material so far.

The focus of this chapter is to get you used to the coordination of moving chord shapes while playing the fingerpicking patterns you've learnt. Your aim with these next exercises should be to change chords smoothly without losing the consistent picking pattern.

Example 2a uses the open E minor chord shape and open G Major:

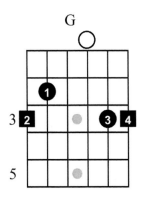

Use the **6 3 2 1** picking pattern. Play the pattern twice for each chord.

Example 2a

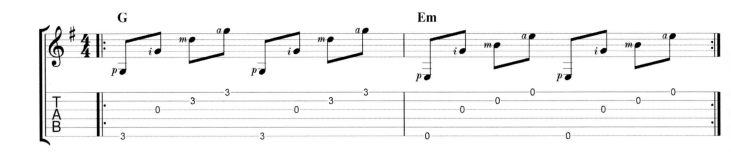

Using the same two chords, change the picking pattern and play **6 1 2 3** twice per bar. You will find that the more you practise these patterns, the more comfortable you'll become at switching between them. Eventually you will be able to seamlessly change between patterns, even within a bar.

Lots of pop songs use these open G Major and E minor chords. Listen to the beginning of *Hero* by Enrique Iglesias, for instance, which uses the **6 1 2 3** pattern.

Example 2b

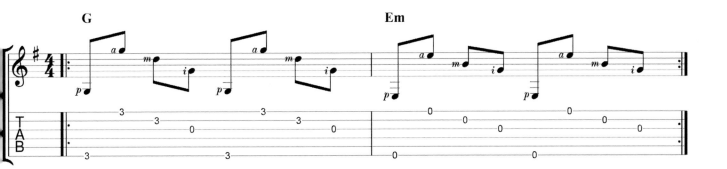

Back in Example 1k I introduced the **6 2 3 1** pattern. This is a popular folk/pop pattern often used by guitarists like James Taylor and John Mayer (I recommend checking out James Taylor's *Greatest Hits* and John Mayer's *Born and Raised* albums). Example 2c applies this pattern to our chord progression.

Example 2c

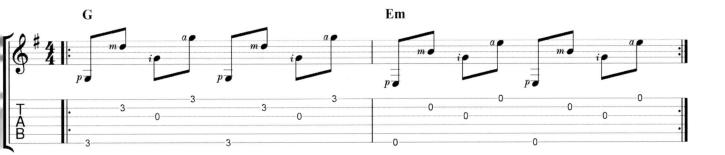

A common technique in acoustic folk music is to pluck two strings at once. You've already practised this technique, but now it's time to apply it to our chord progression. Listen to *Fast Car* by Tracy Chapman to hear how effective this simple technique can be.

Example 2d

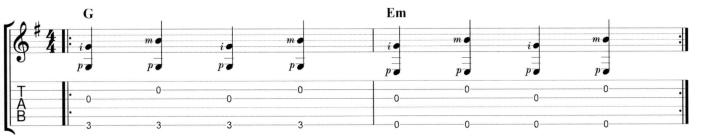

By disciplining the fingers to fingerpick multiple strings at once, you will find more complex patterns easier to play in the future. Example 2e uses the same technique as the previous example, but this time you need to change strings. Keep the bass note going with your thumb while you alternate plucking the B and high E strings (using middle and ring fingers respectively). Listen to *More Than Words* by Extreme for an example of this technique.

Example 2e

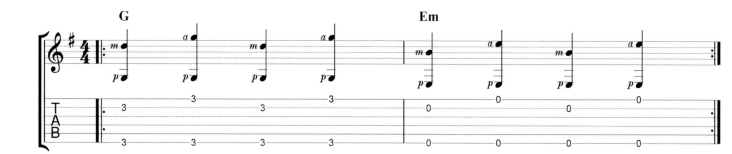

Make sure that you give adequate time to each of the examples in this chapter, as things become progressively more difficult quite quickly! Don't move on until you are able to play the previous examples confidently.

To develop your skills further, Example 2f combines a mixture of single note and multiple note patterns. It's the most complicated thing you've had to play so far, but when you've practised this, you'll really hear the music begin to come to life.

Example 2f

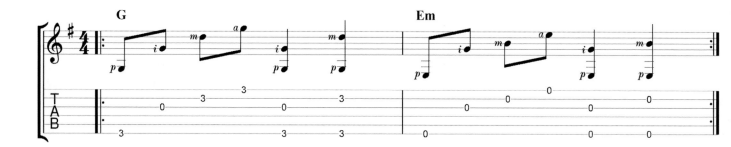

The final two-chord example in this chapter combines single notes and multiple notes in a common pop/folk pattern.

Example 2g

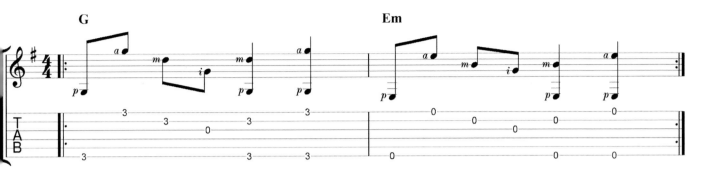

Once you have nailed examples 2f and 2g, experiment with different combinations of the patterns. Take bar one of Example 2f and combine it with bar two of Example 2g, for instance. Treat all of the examples featured in this chapter as a starting point for creating your own preferred patterns.

So far you have learned multiple fingerpicking patterns and how to move between two chord shapes. All the chords have had a root note on the low E string. Any of the examples you've learnt so far will work with any chord with a root on the low E.

Now it's time to practise with chords that have their root note on different strings. The most common ones you'll encounter will have a root note on the 6th (E), 5th (A) and 4th (D) strings (see the table below). When you understand how to move fingerpicking patterns between different strings you will have conquered a big hurdle in fingerstyle guitar. The rest of this chapter will help you solve this!

6th String Root	5th String Root	4th String Root
E Major	A Major	D Major
E Minor	A Minor	D Minor
G Major	C Major	

The examples that follow use a four-chord progression that forms the basis of hundreds of popular songs. For a hilarious video which demonstrates this, search for "Axis of awesome four chords" on YouTube.

Side note: The examples that follow are all in the key of G Major. If you want to move the chord progression into different keys, you can always use a capo. For more advice on using a capo, check out my book *First Chord Progressions for Guitar*.

Four-Chord Progressions

The four-chord progression used in the following examples is G Major – E minor – C Major – D Major. Here are chord grids for the two new chords:

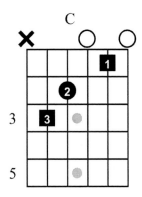

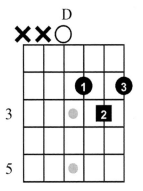

Each chord is played in open position. As you work through the examples, your goal should be to commit to memory each of the fingerpicking patterns. By the end of this chapter you will be able to fingerpick a wide range of well-known tunes.

These examples will help to train your thumb as well as fingers. Until now, you have mostly been picking bass notes on the low E string, but when you play the C Major and D Major chords, you'll be picking bass notes on the fifth (A) and fourth (D) strings respectively. Pay close attention to the notation as you play these examples to ensure you're playing strings with the correct finger.

Let's begin with a simple pattern.

Example 2h uses a **root 3 2 1** pattern and picks through each chord twice per bar. Notice I'm referring to the "root" of the chord now, because the bass note will fall on different strings.

- The root note of the G Major and E minor chords is on the low E string

- The root note of the C Major chord on the fifth string

- The root of the D Major chord on the fourth string

Have a good listen to the audio example before attempting this example. Focus on achieving a smooth transition as you switch strings for the bass notes.

Example 2h

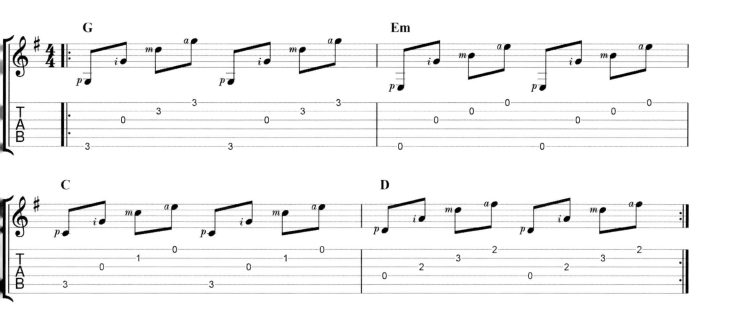

Let's reverse the picking pattern for the fingers and play **root 1 2 3**. Always make sure that you are holding down the chord well while playing, so that all the notes ring out clearly and none of them die away too quickly.

Example 2i

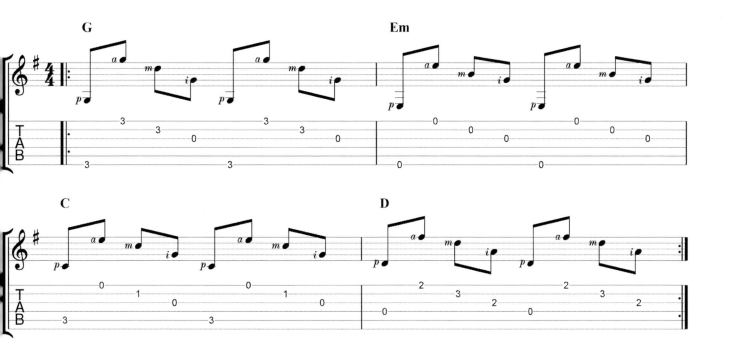

This next example may challenge your coordination, so persevere with it. Play it very slowly to begin with and increase the speed gradually. It's important to lock in that muscle memory. If you don't play it cleanly, when you speed up, you'll still be playing it badly, just quicker!

Here the picking pattern is **root 2 3 1**. You learnt this picking pattern earlier, but now you also have to coordinate moving between bass strings.

Example 2j

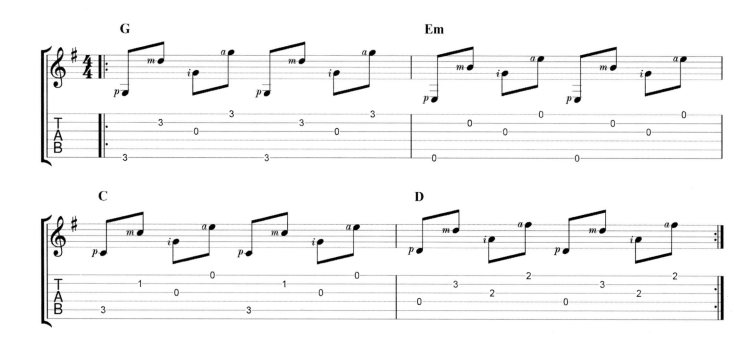

Now it's time to progress to play two notes at a time through the four-chord progression. This exercise will help to develop your picking hand dexterity as the chord voicings for the C and D chords are closer together and greater accuracy is required. Once you have made sure you are playing the pattern correctly, a good way to practise these examples is to sit and watch some TV and drill the pattern over and over again.

The long-term aim is to embed these patterns so that your picking hand plays them automatically with no thought whatsoever. This way you can focus on enjoying playing the music and not worry about the mechanics of the technique.

Example 2k

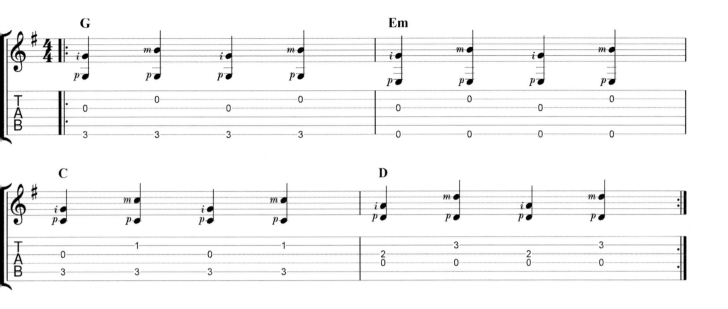

By now, you may be feeling that your ring finger (*a*) seems weaker than your other fingers and thumb. Don't worry, this is completely normal! Patiently work through these exercises and in time you will train it to do what it's told. At any point, return to the exercises in Chapter One to give your ring finger a technical tune-up.

Example 2l has simultaneously plucked notes, but with wider intervals.

Example 2l

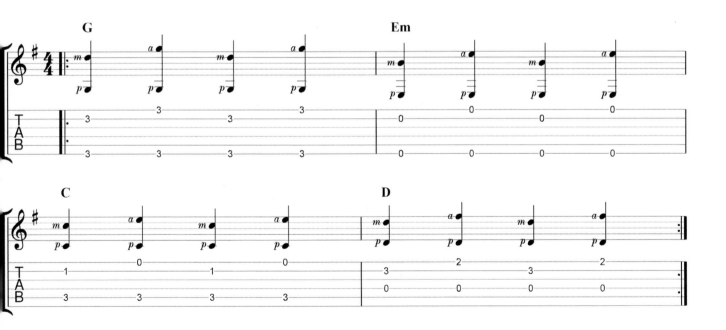

As in previous examples, the next step in the process is to combine individually and simultaneously picked notes – but this time with bass notes moving between strings. Work to get examples 2m and 2n sounding smooth and clean and you will have taken a massive step forward in your fingerpicking journey. Spend as much time in the practice room as you need before moving on.

Example 2m

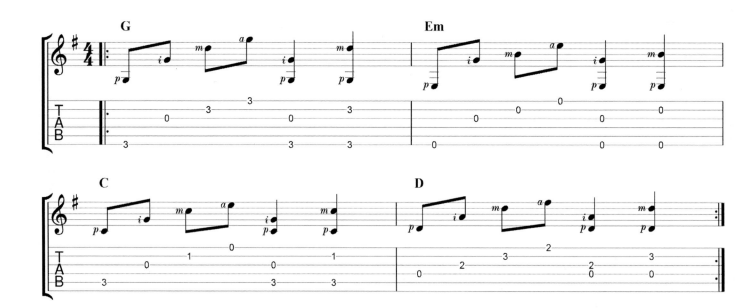

Example 2n

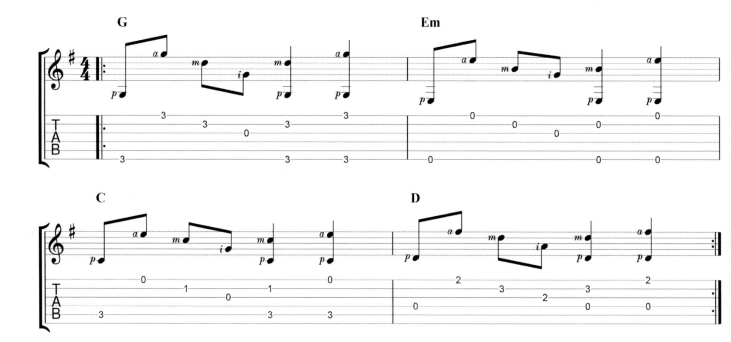

By now you should have become used to the four-chord sequence – G Major, E minor, C Major, D Major – but it's important to learn how to apply picking hand patterns to *any chord sequence*. Let's mix things up by changing the progression slightly. The next two examples in this chapter use the sequence E minor – C Major – G Major – D Major and will help you master changing strings while fingerpicking.

This is another iconic sequence that will sound familiar. Although they will be in different keys to our examples, this progression is used in many famous songs: the chorus of *Let it Be* by the Beatles; the chorus of *Africa* by Toto; *She Will Be Loved* by Maroon 5, and more.

Pay close attention to your picking hand and make sure that as you change shapes, you are picking from the correct string for each chord.

Example 20

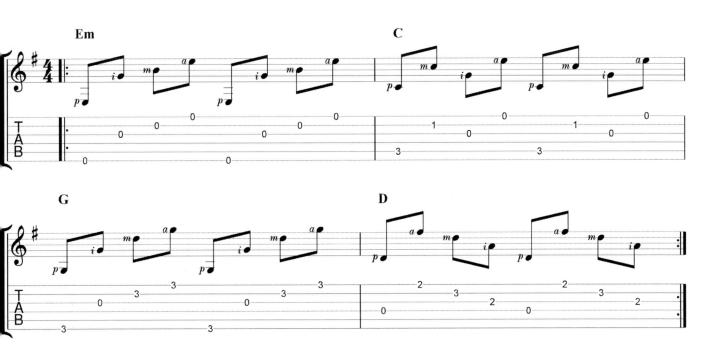

Now combine the single note and two-note patterns learnt earlier and apply them to our new sequence.

Example 2p

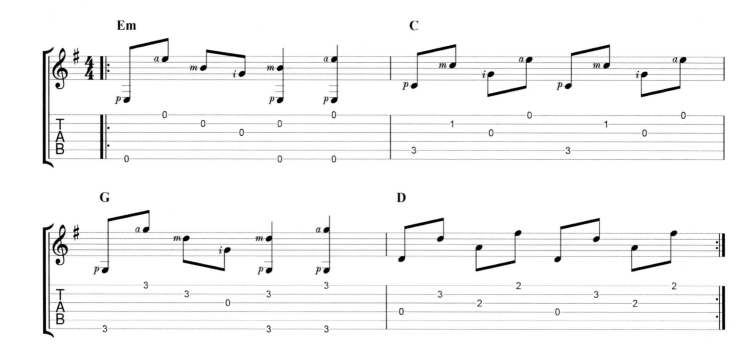

Let's change the order of the chords again, this time to C Major – E minor – D Major – G Major. Example 2q alternates between **root 2 3 1** and **root 1 2 3** patterns.

Example 2q

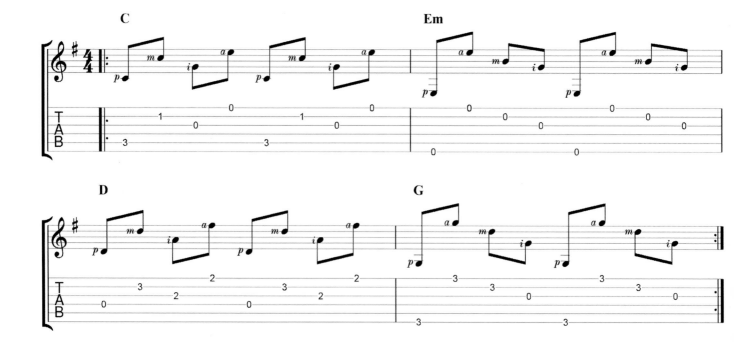

I feel very strongly that it's important to build a repertoire of songs you can play as you work on your fingerpicking technique, so I'll end this chapter with a list of songs that use the progressions you've learnt so far. Listen and play along to them if you can. You'll need to use a capo to play in the same key as the song.

Don't Stop Believing – Journey

You're Beautiful – James Blunt

Where is the Love – Black Eyed Peas

Forever Young – Alphaville

I'm Yours – Jason Mraz

Hey Soul Sister – Train

Wherever You Will Go – The Calling

Can You Feel the Love Tonight – Elton John

Don't Matter – Akon

Take Me Home, Country Roads – John Denver

Paparazzi – Lady Gaga

With or Without You – U2

Pictures of You – The Last Goodnight

She Will Be Loved – Maroon Five

Let it Be – The Beatles

No Woman No Cry – Bob Marley

Land Down Under – Men At Work

Taylor – Jack Johnson

Take On Me – A Ha

When I Come Around – Green Day

Save Tonight – Eagle Eye Cherry

Africa – Toto

Behind These Hazel Eyes – Kelly Clarkson

In my Head – Jason DeRulo

Bullet With Butterfly Wings – The Smashing Pumpkins

One of Us – Joan Osborne

Complicated – Avril Lavigne

Self Esteem – The Offspring

You're Gonna Go Far Kid – The Offspring

Beautiful – Akon

Apologize –One Republic

Love the Way You Lie – Eminem (featuring Rihanna)

It's My Life – Bon Jovi

Pokerface – Lady Gaga

Time To Say Goodbye – Andrea Bocelli

Auld Lang Syne – Robert Burns

Superman – Five for fighting

Chapter Three – Must-Know Folk Picking Patterns

In this chapter you'll learn some of the most popular fingerstyle picking patterns that come from the folk music tradition. These patterns have been passed down from generation to generation over many years and learning them will increase the repertoire of fingerstyle songs you're able to play. We will study them based around familiar chord shapes.

C Shape

The first examples in this chapter are based around an open C Major chord. Notice in the notation below that certain notes should ring out as you play through the pattern. Refer to the audio for these examples to hear how this should sound. It's important to pick each individual note carefully. I recommend setting your metronome to around 50bpm to begin with when playing these examples.

Example 3a features one of the most popular folk fingerstyle patterns for chords with the root note on the A string.

Example 3a

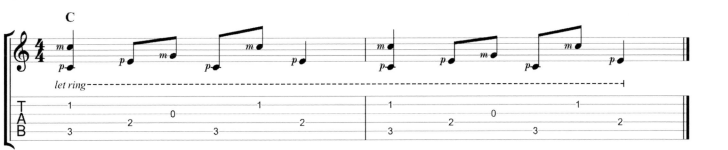

Example 3b varies this pattern by playing the open high E string on the first beat.

Example 3b

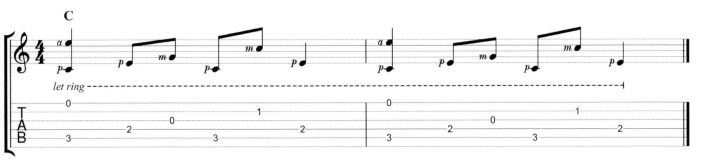

A characteristic of folk patterns is the combination of single note and multiple note (usually two) fingerpicks. The previous example had two notes played on beat 1, but the next example has them on beat 2. Multiple note plucks can occur anywhere in a bar, so experiment with moving them to different beats.

Example 3c

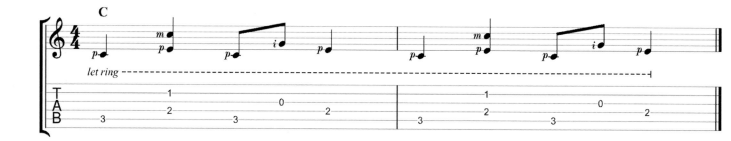

When I was studying at the Guitar Institute, I remember sitting in a fingerstyle guitar class and struggling to make the picking mechanics work. I soon realised that as long as I was playing each pattern with the right fingers – no matter how slowly – I would eventually be able to play them up to speed. It's fine to practice the examples here super-slowly until they are firmly embedded in your muscle memory. I wish someone had told me that at the time!

By now your thumb should be getting well used to alternating between strings. In Example 3d, the ring finger (*a*) will need some careful attention in order to feel comfortable. Don't worry, it's normal for the ring finger to feel the weakest.

Example 3d

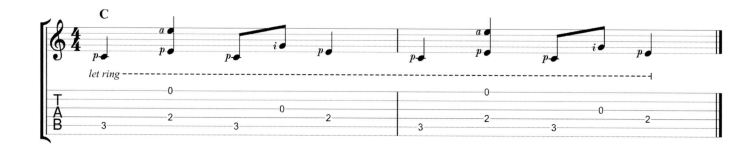

G Shape

It's important to work on fingerpicking mechanics with root notes on different string sets. Now that you feel comfortable with patterns around the C shape, let's move onto patterns around the open G shape with its root on the low E string.

In examples 3e and 3f your thumb will alternate between the notes of G on the low E string, third fret, and the open D string. This also involves a string skip, so it's important to be accurate and not catch the open A string in between. You may want to concentrate on just playing the bass notes cleanly to begin with.

Example 3e

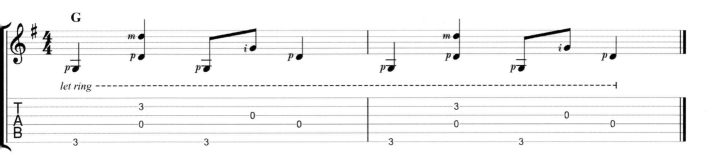

Now let's alter the pattern very slightly. Example 3f is identical to the previous example, except you pluck the high E string on beat 2.

Example 3f

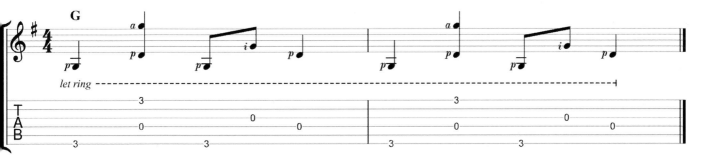

It's time to learn a new idea now, which is related to our open G chord. It's very common – especially in modern pop ballads – to play a chord with a bass note that isn't the root. In bar two of Example 3g below, the chord is notated G/B. This means it's a G chord with a B note in the bass and it looks like this:

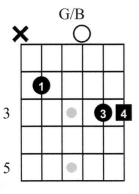

Chords like this are commonly called "slash chords" (two notes separated by a slash) and songwriters use them all the time to create nice movements in the bassline. The G/B chord is often used after a plain G chord has been played. Although it's played in a different key, you can hear this chord change in Ed Sheeran's *Thinking Out Loud* and many other tunes.

Side note: For more information about slash chords, check out my video lesson on **www.fundamental-changes.com**

G/B is also used as a passing chord to move between C Major and A minor, as in Example 3g. This is a longer example, so as ever, take it slowly to begin with. Accuracy of picking rather than speed is the goal.

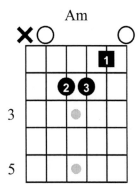

Example 3g

D Shape

Next is the D shape. With the root note on the open D string, this chord shape is more closely arranged and it's easy for your fingers to get in each other's way, so keep an eye on your positioning.

Picking the open D string with the thumb while simultaneously picking the high E string with your ring finger is the trickiest part of Example 3h and can feel a little unnatural to begin with. Practice this motion on its own to begin with, before playing the whole thing.

Example 3h

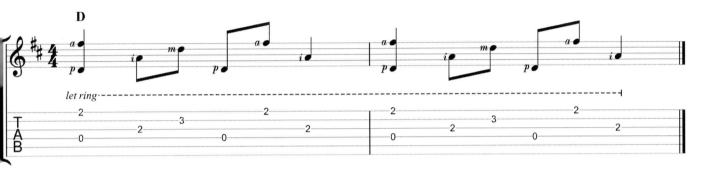

Example 3i presents another challenge: plucking the G and high E strings simultaneously with the index and ring fingers. With the thumb and fingers so close together, there is the temptation to let the thumb jump onto the G string, but you mustn't let the thumb do the index finger's job!

There are some great tunes you should check out that use the open D Major chord. John Mayer favours it in his version of *Free Fallin'* by Tom Petty, and his tunes *Who Says* and *Stop This Train* are excellent examples of how to use it in context.

Example 3i

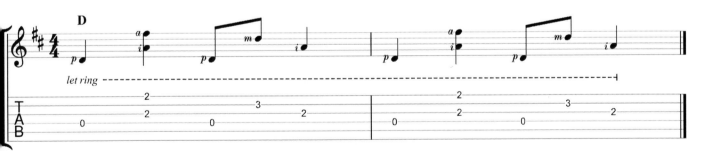

Fingerpicking More Than Two Notes at a Time

Until now, the examples have required you to pluck no more than two notes simultaneously. To move things forward, the next examples will develop your ability to pluck groups of three or four notes at the same time.

For Example 3j, fret an open C Major chord. On the first beat, pluck strings 5, 3, 2 and 1 at the same time. The motion you make with your picking hand will be a bit like grasping a small object, with your thumb moving down towards your fingers. On beat 2, leave out the bass note on string 5 and just pluck the top three strings. On beat 3 pluck strings 4, 3, 2 and 1, and just strings 3, 2 and 1 on the last beat.

Again, don't worry if this feel awkward at first. The mechanical skills of picking and plucking take time to develop and this is completely normal.

Example 3j

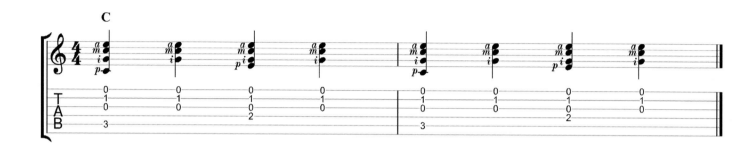

Now let's apply the multiple fingerpick technique to an open G chord shape. For ease, here's a simple chart to show which strings you should be plucking.

Beat 1: 6, 3, 2, 1

Beat 2: 3, 2, 1

Beat 3: 5, 3, 2, 1

Beat 4: 3, 2, 1

Example 3k

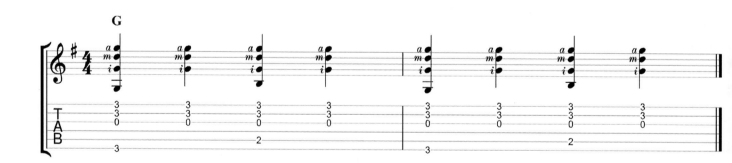

Example 3l combines the previous two examples and also introduces a new chord. Its complicated name might look intimidating, but it's actually very easy to play. You just need to move your open C Major shape up two frets to create the lovely, ringing D chord shape in bar three.

A simple plucking pattern like this works really well when backing a vocalist or playing in a duo with another musician. Often, a lovely fingerstyle pattern can sound a lot more intricate than a simple strumming pattern.

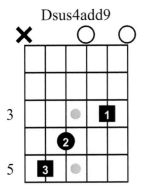

Dsus4add9

Example 3l

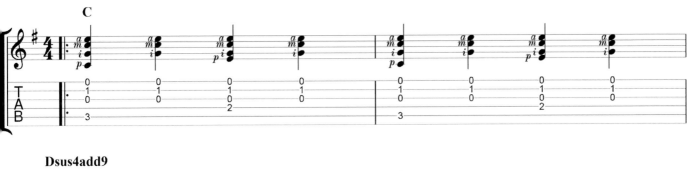

Dsus4add9

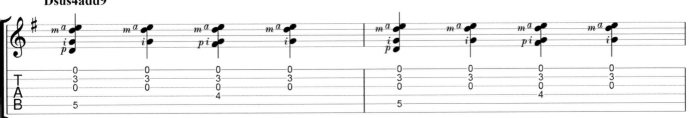

G

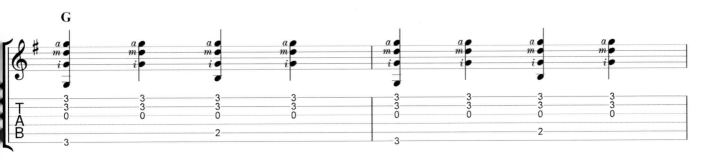

G

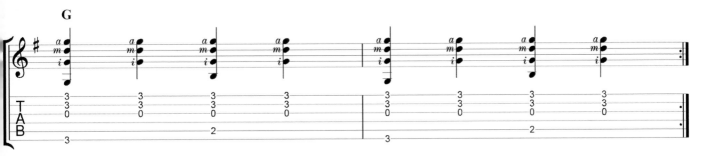

More Complex Patterns

We've already explored how different folk fingerstyle picking patterns can be mixed and matched to create new ones. Really, the options are endless, and it comes down to what appeals to you. Always experiment and explore your own options. You can achieve this by combining any of the examples seen in this chapter.

The next examples build on all that you've learnt so far to create more variety and more complex sounding patterns. Here we have a combination of wide interval picking and plucking more than one note at once. Examples 3m and 3n do this with the open C Major chord shape. Try to let each note ring out as much as possible when playing them and listen to the audio examples.

Example 3m

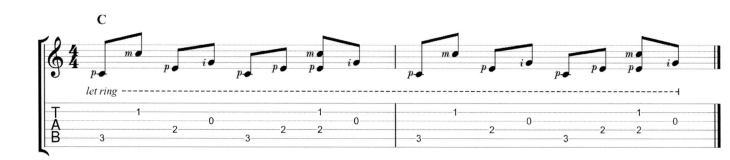

Example 3n

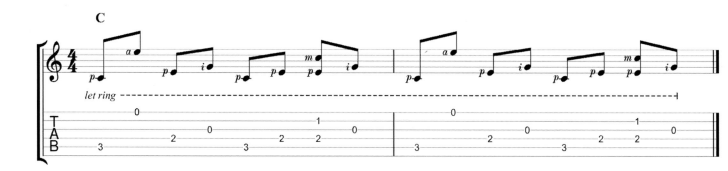

When you feel comfortable applying these patterns to the C shape, you can apply them to an open G Major chord. A great way to learn and embed these patterns is to get a chord chart for a song you really like, and play the chords using one of the example picking patterns. It's one thing to develop your technique, but you also want to be able to play recognisable songs.

Example 3o

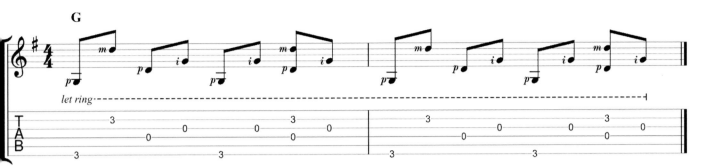

Example 3p

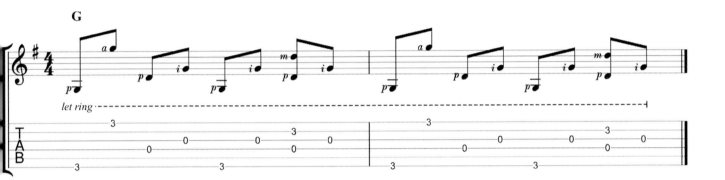

Now let's apply this picking pattern to the open D Major chord shape. It's important to apply any new picking pattern you learn to chords with root notes on the 6th, 5th *and* 4th strings.

Example 3q

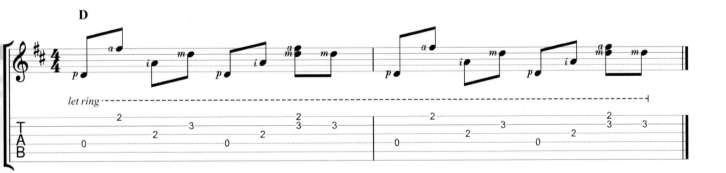

Earlier we encountered our first slash chord (a chord with a different note than the root in the bass). Example 3r introduces a new slash chord: a D Major chord with an F# bass note. Here's a diagram to show you how to play the full chord, along with a useful grip for playing the Em7 voicing.

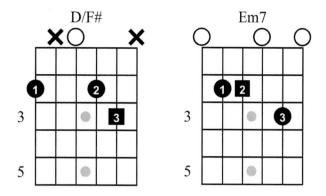

This shape is extremely popular and works especially well when moving between the chords of G Major and E minor, as it creates a nice descending bassline. Make sure you let the notes ring out as indicated below.

Example 3r

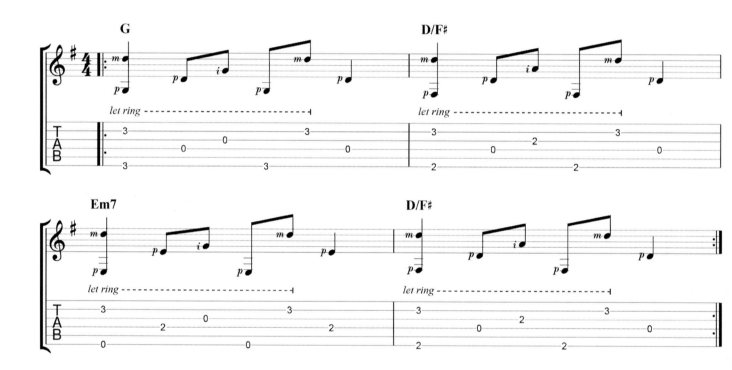

It's important to take time to really get comfortable with all you've learnt so far. We've covered a lot of ground already and the most important thing is to embed the picking technique and patterns into your muscle memory. Don't feel you need to rush ahead.

For those readers who are ready for the next challenge, I've included two longer pieces for you to dissect and learn. There are videos of both these pieces on the Fundamental Changes website, so you can see how they are performed. You can watch them here:

www.fundamental-changes.com/beginner-acoustic-videos

The first piece is called *September's Breeze*. It is in the key of C Major and uses a classic folk fingerstyle pattern that will likely sound very familiar to you. There are no big surprises here, just the inclusion of the G/B slash chord. If you've worked through this chapter sequentially, then the chord shapes and fingerpicking patterns should feel comfortable to you.

September's Breeze

Example 3s

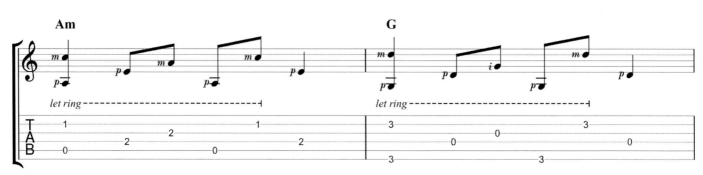

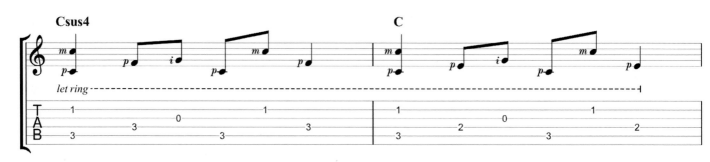

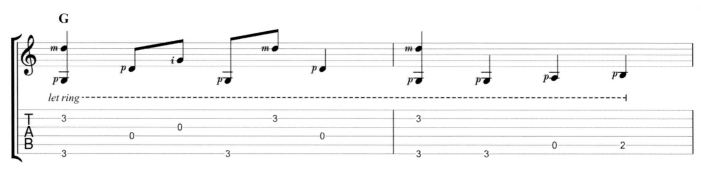

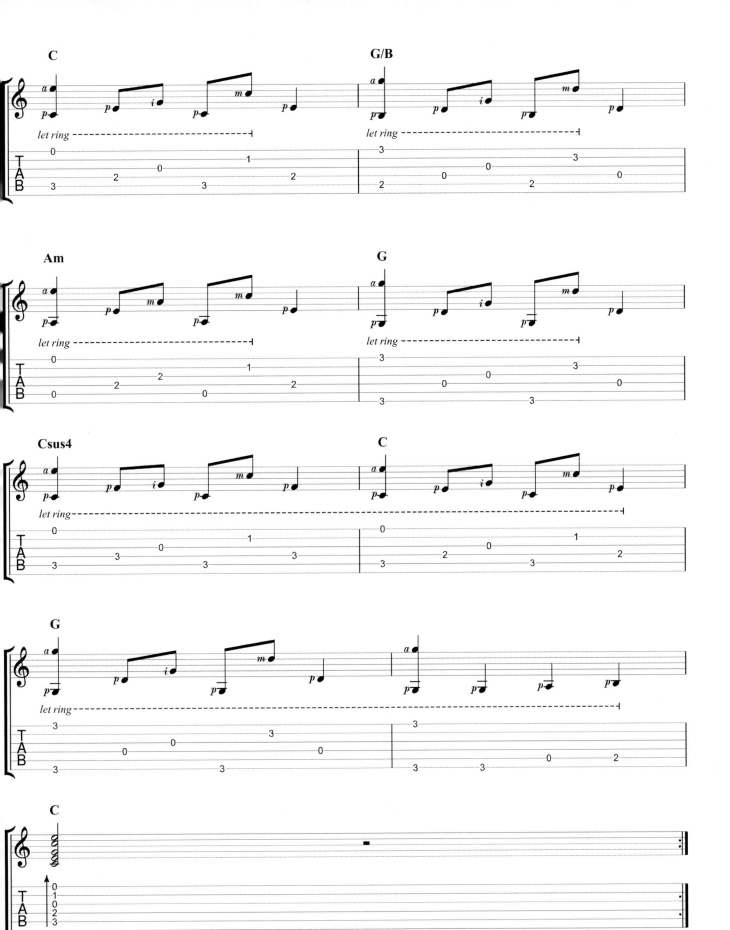

The second piece is called *Still Here*. It is in the key of E minor and uses the chords Em, Cadd9, G and D. These are common open chords, but the chord shapes used here are slightly different to normal. Below are chord grids for the special voicings:

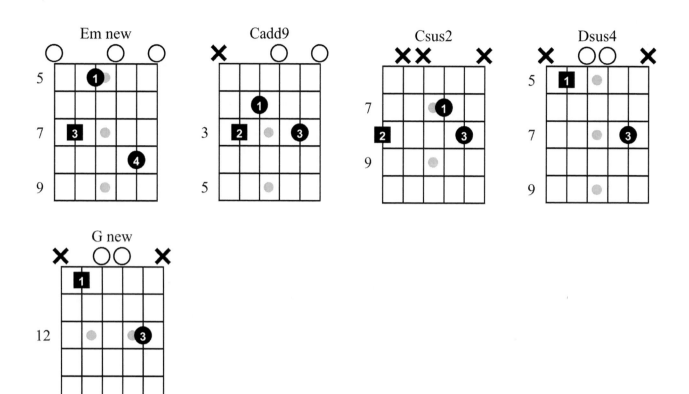

Watch the performance video before attempting this piece:

www.fundamental-changes.com/beginner-acoustic-videos

Still Here

Example 3t

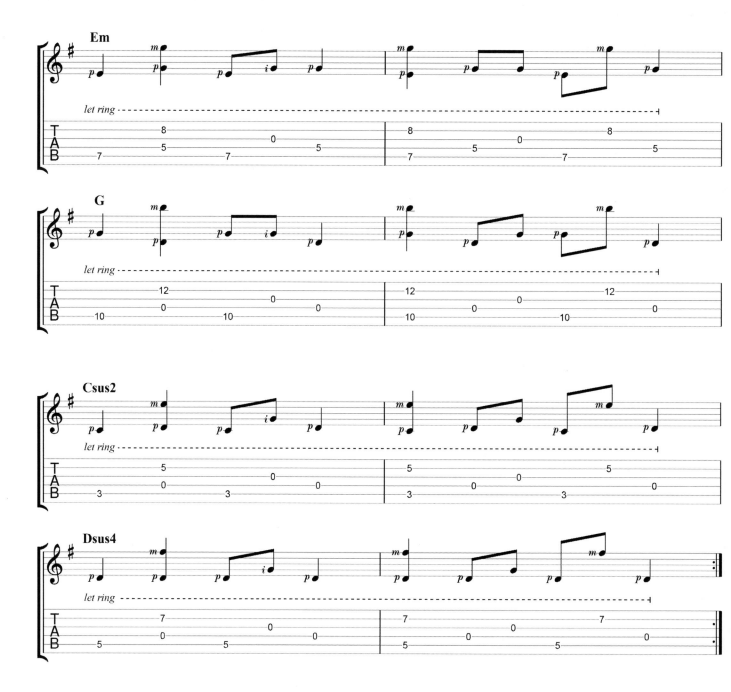

Now that you've completed this chapter, it's a good idea to check out some classic tunes that feature iconic fingerpicked guitar parts. Get hold of a chord chart for any tune you like and see if you can work out what picking pattern is being used. There are a wealth of songs out there but listen to these for starters: *Dear Prudence* by The Beatles, *Dust in the Wind* by Kansas, *Tears in Heaven* by Eric Clapton, or for something more challenging, *Stop This Train* by John Mayer.

Chapter Four – Mini-Chords

In the chapters that follow, we're going to explore some simple but effective new ideas to take your fingerstyle guitar playing to the next level. The first of these is a favourite topic of mine that I've taught to many students over the years, which I like to call *mini-chords*.

One of the great myths of fingerstyle guitar is that you need to play difficult, complex chords to create a full sounding arrangement. In reality, it's surprising how *little* you need to play to create a lovely, full sounding accompaniment or performance piece.

One of the major advantages of fingerstyle guitar technique compared to using a pick, is that you can pluck non-adjacent strings simultaneously, with ease. This creates a very different sound to either straight-ahead strumming or typical folk picking patterns.

Have a listen to the introduction of the tunes *Hold Back the River* by James Bay and *Many of Horror (When We Collide)* by Biffy Clyro. Also check out *Blackbird* by The Beatles. All these tunes use *mini-chords* that only require you to fret *two notes*.

Let's have a look at some of these mini-chord shapes. We'll look at the chord shapes with root notes on strings 6, 5 and 4 in turn, and you'll learn some nice ideas you can play with them.

6th String Shapes

Example 4a shows how to create a two-note G Major shape with its root note on the low E string. Without getting bogged down in too much theory, this chord shape is referred to as a 10th voicing. It's made up from the root (a G note) and the 3rd (a B note). The interval of a 3rd is what defines a chord as being major or minor. In this chord shape, the B note has been moved up an octave, so the 3rd is now described as a 10th.

What's great about these simple voicings is that with just two notes you can spell out the essential flavour of the chord. Try them out!

NB: *Play all these examples by plucking simultaneously with the thumb and the appropriate finger for the higher string.*

Example 4a

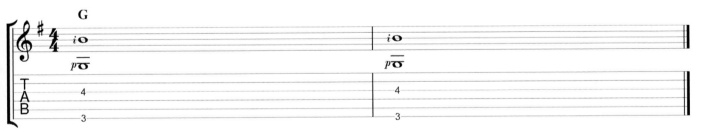

It's very simple to turn this G Major voicing into a G minor chord. The 3rd interval (B) is lowered a semitone to become a b3 (Bb). The root and b3 combination spell out a G minor chord.

Example 4b

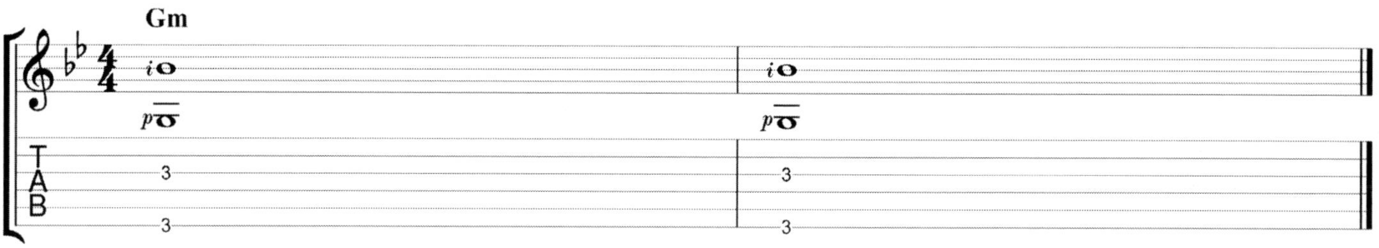

5th String Shapes

Next, let's examine some useful mini-chord shapes with their root note on the A string. Example 4c is a C Major chord.

Example 4c

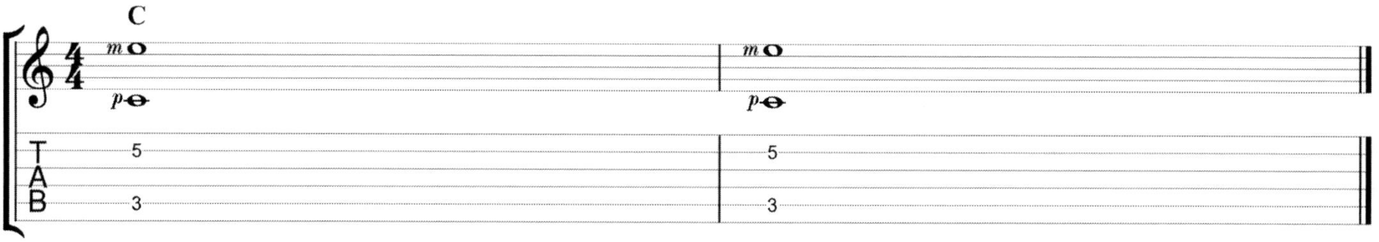

As before, by lowering the top note by a semitone, the chord becomes C minor.

Example 4d

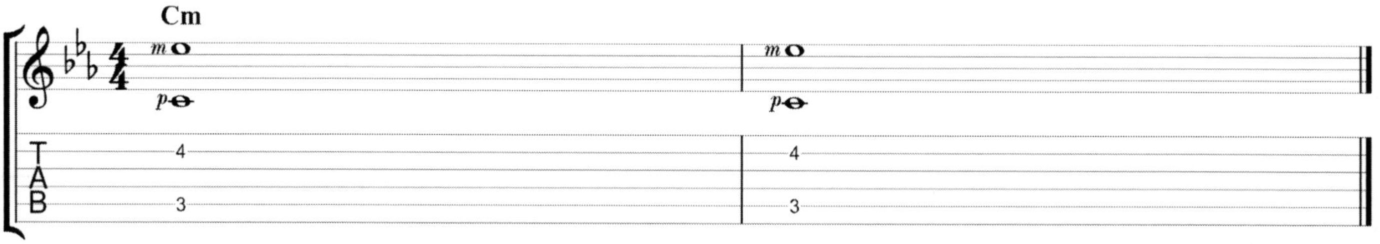

4th String Shapes

Finally, we have major and minor mini-chord shapes with their root on the D string. First, here is an F Major chord.

Example 4e

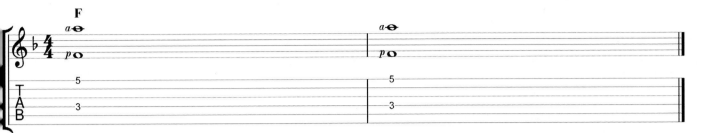

And the corresponding F minor chord:

Example 4f

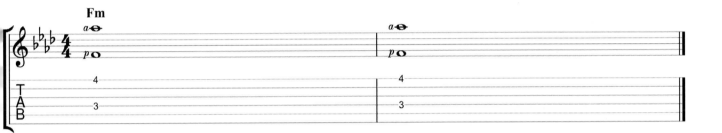

Play through these shapes a few times to familiarise yourself with their position on the fretboard and experiment moving them around the neck. Once you can jump to the major/minor shapes on each string set, it's time to explore what can be done with them in the following examples.

Example 4g may remind you of the Beatles' tune *Blackbird*, as that song was written in the key of G Major and used similar mini-chord shapes. As you play this example, you'll notice that the strings you are *not* playing resonate in a lovely way, which adds to the overall effect and creates a fuller sound.

Example 4g

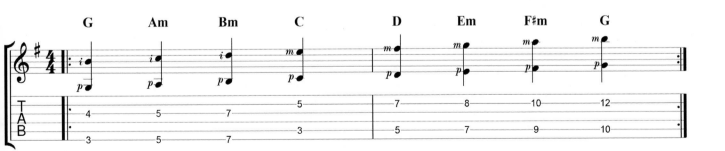

A great way to really learn a pattern is to play it descending as well as ascending, so here is Example 4g played in reverse.

Example 4h

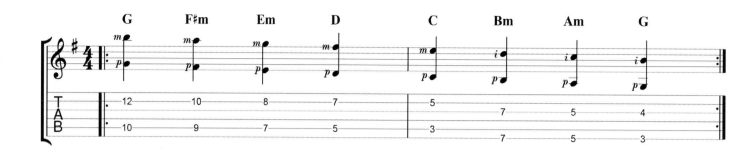

Play through examples 4g and 4h several times until the shapes become second nature to you. Once you feel comfortable with them, you can begin to add small embellishments between the chords. Example 4i is a very effective way to play a progression in G Major using mini-chords and applies a simple picking pattern. The pattern is identical for each chord, so once you learn it you can focus on changing smoothly between the chord shapes.

Example 4i

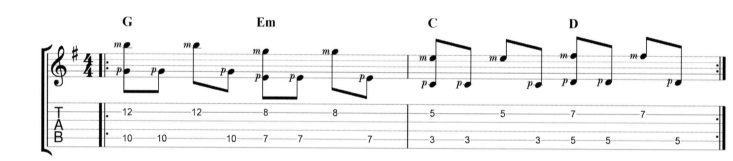

Example 4j applies this pattern to a slightly different progression in G Major.

Example 4j

Another useful pattern is to play two chord plucks followed by just the root note of the chord. A great tune to learn that uses this approach is *Fast Car* by Tracy Chapman.

Example 4k

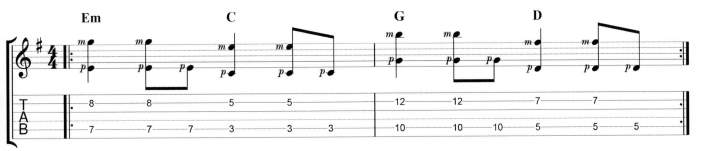

Example 4l shows how effective it can be to include an open string in between 10th mini-chord voicings. It works particularly well in the key of G Major where we're able to play the open G string.

Example 4l

The next example shows how you can combine a mini-chord, bass note and open string to create a lush-sounding picking pattern.

Example 4m

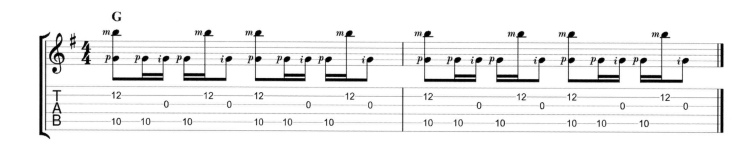

Now let's apply this more complex picking pattern to a progression. Set your metronome to a comfortable 50bpm and keep your picking pattern consistent as you move through the chord changes. Only raise the tempo when you can complete this example perfectly five times in a row!

Example 4n

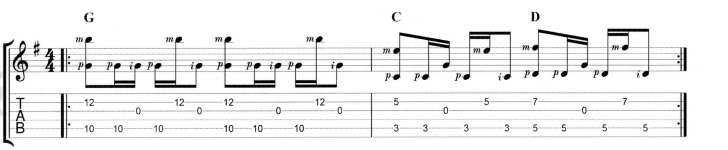

Let's change the progression again but keep the picking pattern going. This style of fingerpicking works especially well when backing a vocalist in a duo setting, and is often used in a contemporary worship or Gospel setting too.

Example 4o

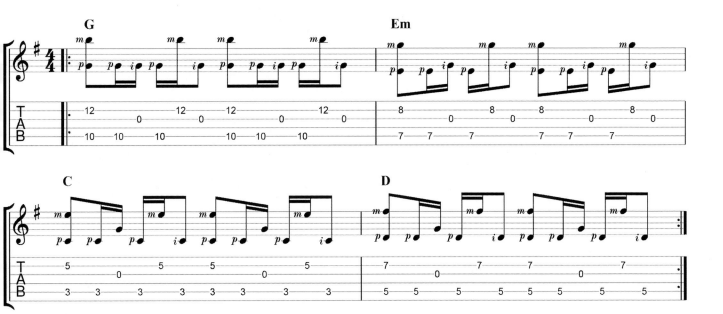

The great thing about these mini-chord shapes is that they sound brilliant whether played slow or fast. When you are comfortable with the shapes and picking patterns, try them at faster tempos, but don't sacrifice accuracy for speed.

To end, here is a simple example that uses less common mini-chords with a root on the D string.

Example 4p

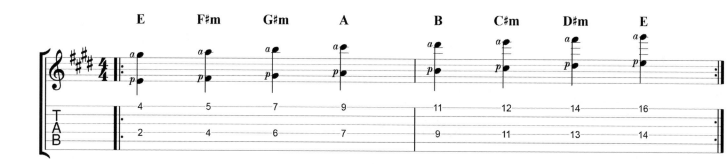

Mini-chords with their root on the D string sound a little more delicate than their E and A string counterparts, and can be very useful when you want to play a light accompaniment.

Chapter Five – Adding Embellishments to Major Chords

In the previous chapter we discovered that it's possible to create some beautiful chord progressions using simple two-note mini-chords. Over the course of the next two chapters I want to show you some simple tricks to add embellishments to open major and minor chords.

You might think that the techniques of hammer-ons and pull-offs are only used by rock guitarists, but in fact they are great tools to add movement and excitement to acoustic fingerstyle guitar arrangements. We are going to look at some simple ways of incorporating this *legato* effect into your fingerstyle playing. To hear the heights this technique can be taken to, check out the tune *Summer Breeze* by Martin Tallstrom.

In this chapter we'll add embellishments to major chords, and in Chapter Six we'll work with minor chords.

All these embellishments are presented as melodic ideas to explore around one chord at a time. This helps with organisation, but it isn't the most musical way to learn the ideas. Instead of learning each idea in isolation, I highly recommend that you learn one idea around one chord, then apply it to a chord sequence. You can either try to adapt an idea to fit around the other chords or learn a separate idea to play on each chord and then combine them. I've written five chord sequences below which can serve as a framework for learning the embellishments in a musical context.

Make sure you can play the basic chord sequences fluently before you add any embellishments.

1)

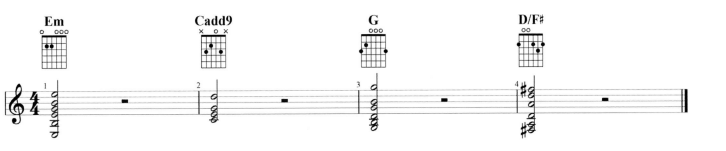

2)

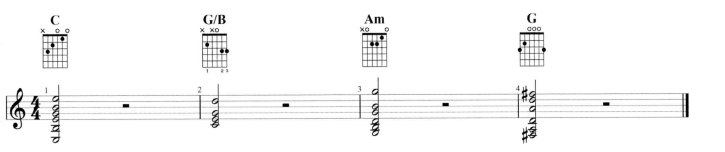

3)

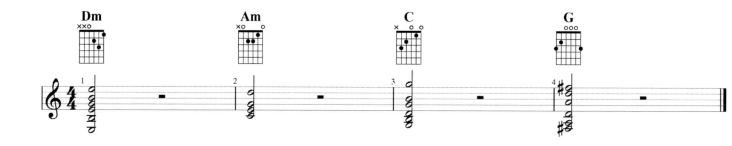

4)

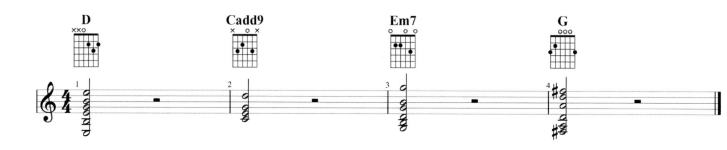

5)

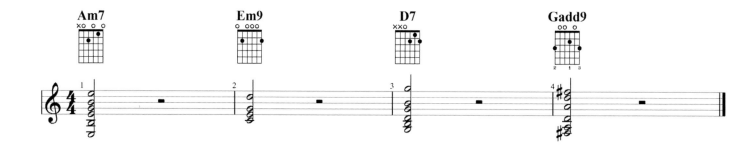

Hammer-Ons

The first six examples are all based around an open C Major chord shape. The other notes, added to create the legato effect, come from the C Major scale (C, D, E, F, G, A, B).

In Example 5a, pick through the C Major chord from the A to high E strings. On the D string you will pick the open D note, then hammer-on to the second fret. You only need to pluck the string once – it's your fretting hand middle finger that does the work of sounding the additional note.

Example 5a

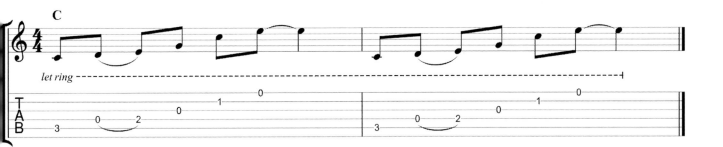

Now play the chord again, but this time place the hammer-on on the B string, hammering from the open B to the first fret.

Example 5b

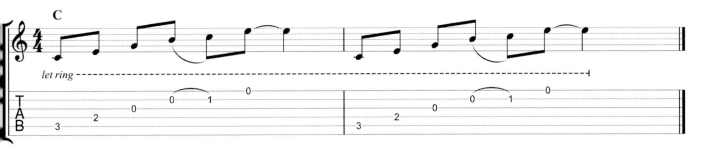

Example 5c combines the two previous examples to create an interesting legato C Major chord pattern. As you play it, let all the notes ring into each other.

Example 5c

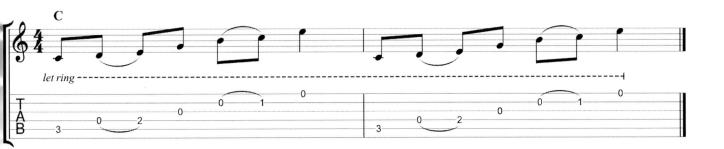

As well as hammering-on from open strings you can hammer-on from fretted notes too. You may find the hammer-on in Example 5d a touch more difficult, as you will be using your 1st and 4th fingers to complete it. Fret the open C Major chord shape and just work on the hammer-on before adding in the rest of the fingerpicking pattern.

Example 5d

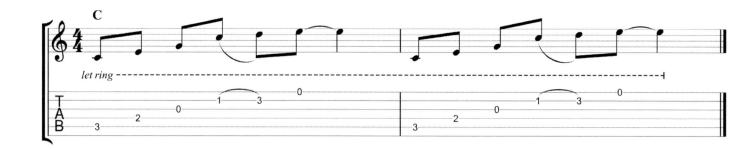

Pull-Offs

When you feel comfortable fretting a chord shape and adding hammer-ons, you can do the reverse, adding some pull-off patterns to the C Major chord shape. To execute a pull-off, you fret the desired note then pull you finger away from the string, towards the floor. This downward motion causes the string to sound.

Example 5e descends through the C Major chord. You will pluck the D string with your thumb, then pull-off with your fretting hand middle finger.

Example 5e

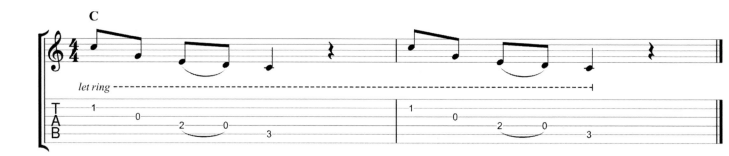

Example 5f is also a descending idea and this time the pull-off occurs at the beginning on the B string, executed by pulling-off with your first finger.

Example 5f

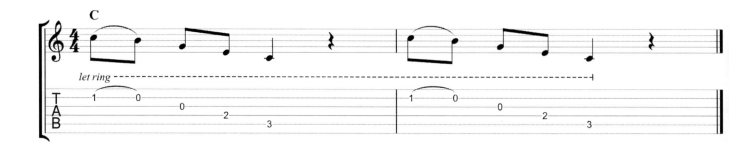

The next pull-off from the third to first fret on the B string is executed by the pinky finger.

Example 5g

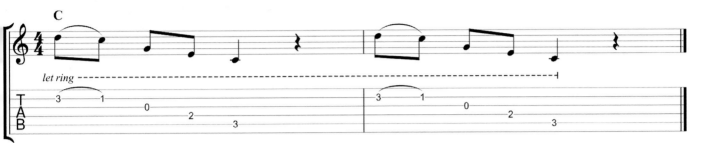

Now let's see where this idea can take us – combining hammer-ons and pull-offs around the open C Major chord. If you've worked through the examples sequentially so far, then you'll be able to play Example 5h if you approach it slowly and with care. It demonstrates a free-flowing two-bar legato pattern.

Example 5h

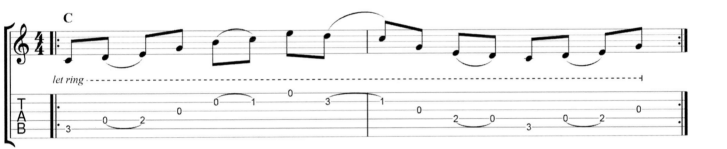

G Major Hammer-On Patterns

Now it's time to look at some common legato embellishments to the open G Major chord shape. The legato fills used around the G Major chord come from the G Major scale (G, A, B, C, D, E, F#).

We approach it in the same way as before, discovering the nice sounding notes located around the chord. In Example 5i, hold down the G chord shape. You'll find it easier to then lift off your fretting hand index finger from the A string before you play the chord, to get ready to play the hammer-on.

Example 5i

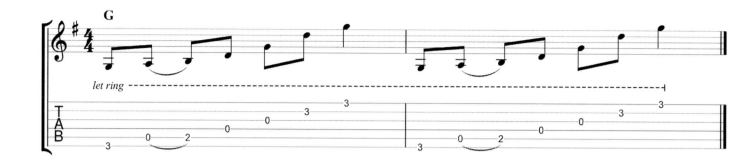

The next hammer-on pattern we can add to the G Major chord shape is an open D string to second fret hammer-on. This is the first hammer-on idea that requires a string change with the fretting hand. As you hold down the chord, your index finger will be fretting the second fret note on the A string. After you pluck the A string with your thumb, move your index finger across to play the hammer-on on the D string.

Example 5j

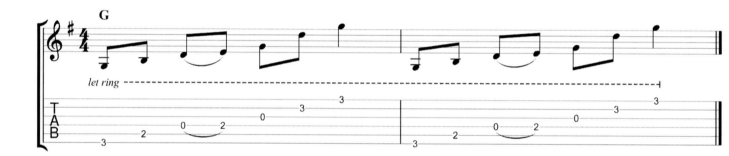

Example 5k moves the hammer-on to the open G string. You need to play the hammer-on with your index finger again, and this time it involves skipping over a string to do it. Take it slowly and make sure you can execute it cleanly before speeding up.

Example 5k

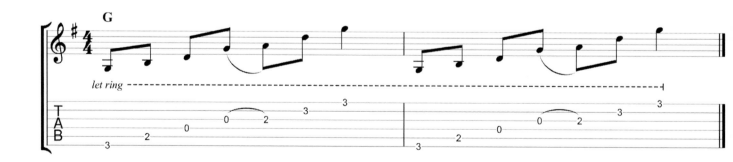

The next example moves the hammer-on to the B string. The hammer-on is played with the ring finger this time. It can feel awkward to lift off just the ring finger when you're fretting the full chord. It's a little easier to lift off both ring finger and pinky, play the open B string, and place both fingers back down at the same time.

Example 5l

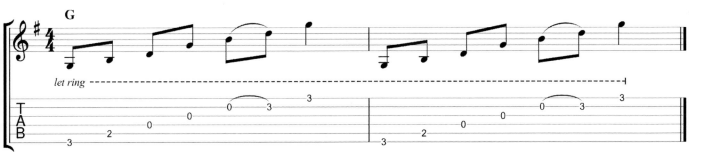

Lastly, the hammer-on can be played on the high E string. This time it's easier to hold the full chord and just lift the pinky off to play the hammer-on.

Example 5m

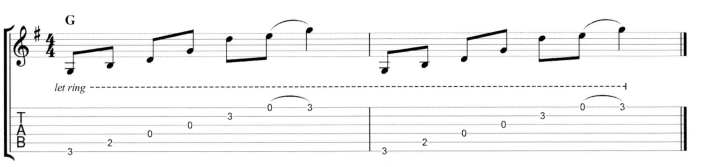

G Major Pull-Off Patterns

Now let's work through the pull-off patterns around the G Major chord. First, we have a descending idea with a pull-off from the second fret to open A string. You'll play the pull-off with your index finger.

Example 5n

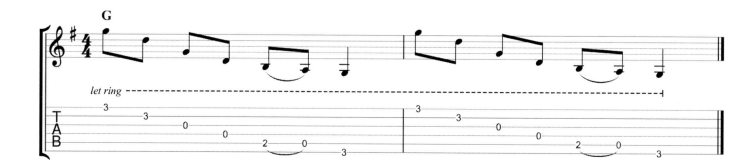

Now we move the pull-off to the D string. This is played with the index finger and you'll need to hop across a string as you did before, but in reverse. After playing the hammer-on, move your index finger to the A string, second fret.

Example 5o

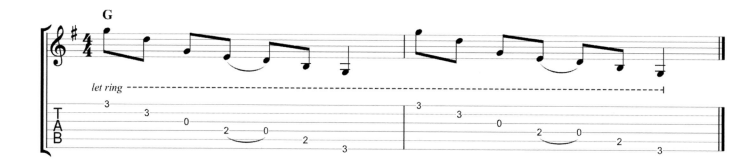

The next example has the pull-off on the B string. Like the earlier hammer-on example, this needs to be executed with the ring finger, and it's easier to lift up both the ring finger and pinky after playing the high E string.

Example 5p

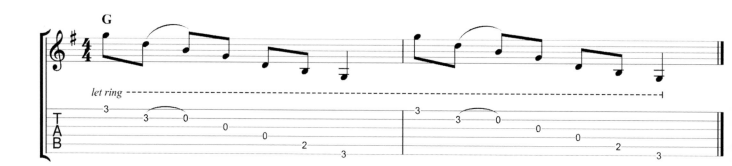

Finally, we move the pull-off to the high E string, played with the pinky.

Example 5q

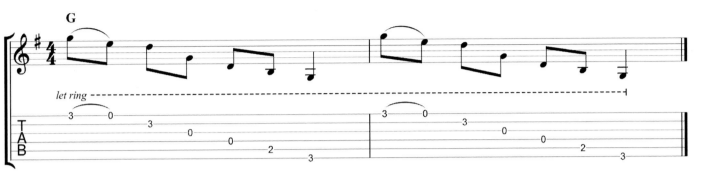

Combining Hammer-Ons And Pull-Offs Around the Open G Major Chord

Now let's bring these ideas together in a two-bar example around the G Major chord shape.

Example 5r blends legato notes together around the open G shape using the G Major Pentatonic scale (G A B D E). This pattern is frequently used in country and folk songs, but also appears in pop and rock music.

Example 5r

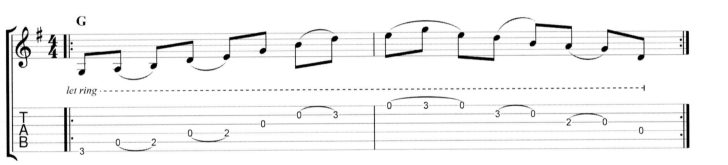

D Major Hammer-On Patterns

The next chord shape is the open D Major shape. Like the previous shapes, there are some common legato patterns to learn. These will be based around the D Major scale (D E F# G A B C#).

Example 5s is one of the most common embellishments. Fret the open D Major shape and fingerpick from the D to the high E string. On the high E string, hammer-on from the open string to the second fret with your middle finger.

Example 5s

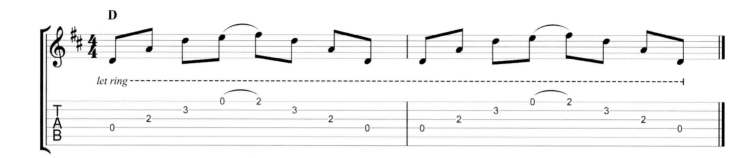

Next we move the hammer-on to the G string, played with the index finger.

Example 5t

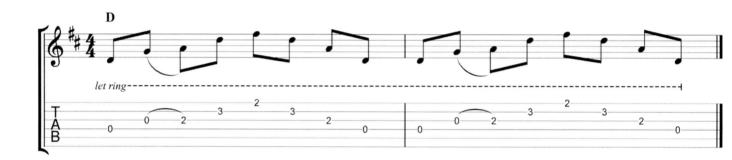

Example 5u takes a slightly different approach. To play this idea it's easiest to barre your index finger across the G, B and high E strings at the second fret. Played with a straight strum this forms a Dmaj7 chord. Hold the barre and hammer-on to the third fret of the B string with your ring finger.

Example 5u

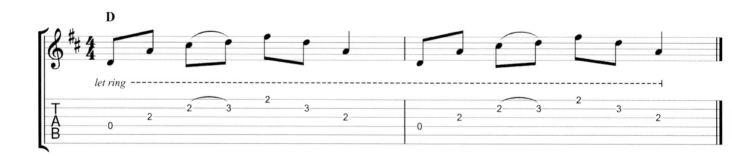

Example 5v features a pull-off from the third to second fret on the high E string. This is a very popular embellishment on a D chord and creates the sound of a Dsus4 chord moving to the D Major.

Example 5v

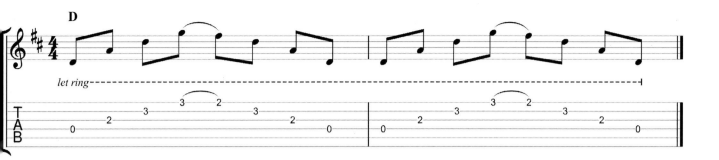

For Example 5w, barre the G, B and E strings as before and hammer-on to the high E string fifth fret with your pinky finger.

Example 5w

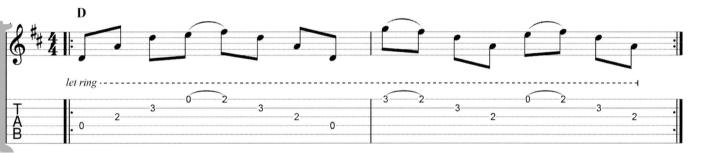

Let's combine some of these ideas into a two-bar phrase. Here is a fun pattern I use a lot in my playing.

Example 5x

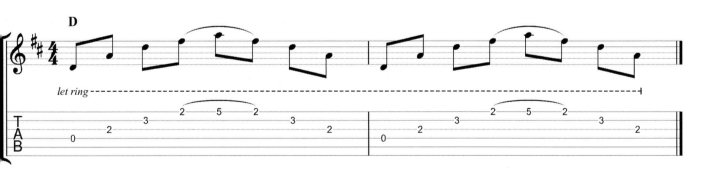

A Major Legato Patterns

For the final examples in this chapter, we'll apply what we've learnt to an open A Major chord, skipping right ahead to some two-bar examples. The added notes will come from the A Major scale (A, B, C#, D, E, F#, G#).

Open A Major can be played a few different ways, and players tend to settle on their preferred method. If you've been playing this chord the same way for years, you may find it easier to adjust it in order to play some of the legato patterns that follow.

For Example 5y I recommend holding down the chord using your first finger. It will make the hammer-on and pull-off feel much more comfortable.

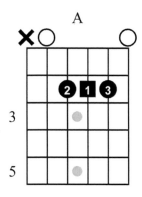

Example 5y

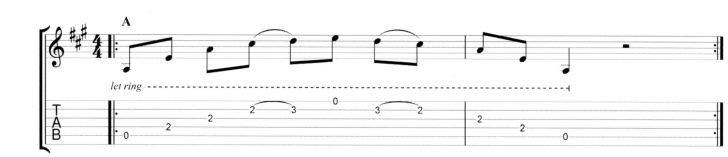

In the next example, the hammer-on and pull-off are executed by the index finger on the D string.

Example 5z

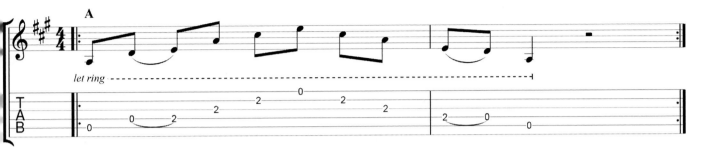

For Example 5za, it's easier to perform this legato line by holding down the D string second fret with your middle finger, with your index finger fretting the G string first fret (in preparation for the hammer-on). Keeping these fingers in place, hammer-on to the G string second fret with your ring finger. Then, keeping the ring finger in place, hammer-on from the open B string to the second fret with your pinky.

All your fingers should be on the fretboard now! As you descend back down the strings, you'll remove your pinky them middle finger to execute the pull-offs.

Check out Peppino D'Agostino's *Born in The Sea* as a great example of this technique!

Example 5za

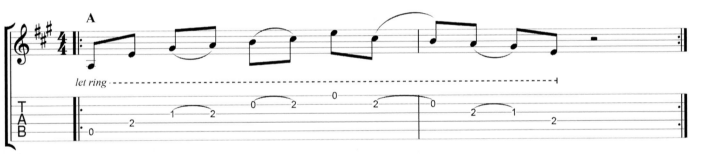

The final example of this chapter combines several different A Major legato patterns into one idea. I find this example easiest to play fretting the A Major chord shape with fingers two, three and four.

Example 5zb

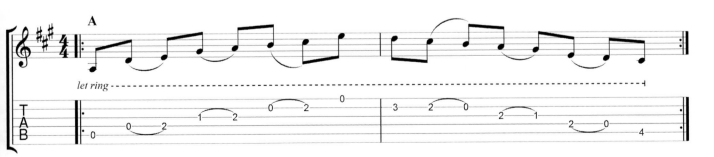

We've covered many different ways in which you can decorate simple open major chord shapes to spice up your fingerstyle playing. Now you've learnt some useful patterns, why not try experimenting with a capo to play them in different keys? I personally love the sound of the capo at the third or fourth frets and it's amazing how transferring ideas to other keys affects how they sound. Experiment and get creative with it.

Chapter Six – Adding Embellishments to Minor Chords

In the previous chapter we discovered how to add legato embellishments to major chord shapes. In this chapter we'll apply the same principles to minor chord shapes.

A Minor Legato Patterns

We begin with this popular open A minor chord shape. The added notes will come from the A Natural Minor scale (A B C D E F G).

The first example is an easy hammer-on from the open D string to the second fret using the middle finger. Allow the notes to ring into each other as much as possible.

Example 6a

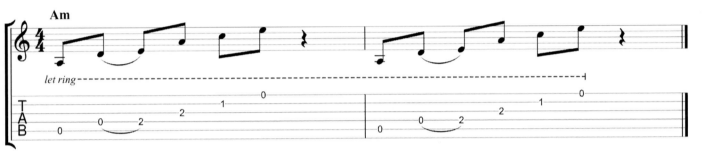

Another common move is to hammer-on from the open G string to the second fret with the ring finger.

Example 6b

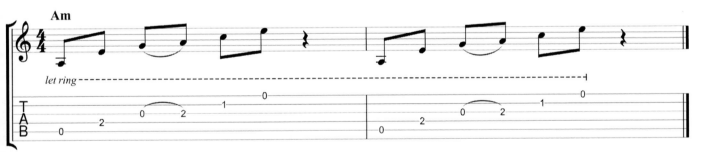

Another easy but effective move is to hammer-on from the open B string to the first fret with the index finger.

Example 6c

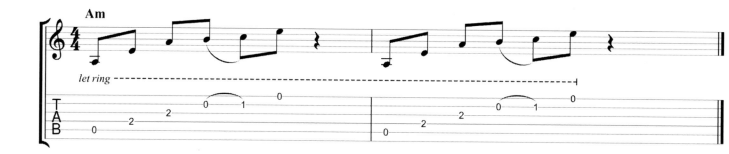

Example 6d demonstrates a nice embellishment played by holding the A minor chord in place and hammering onto the B string third fret with the pinky finger. After playing the hammer-on you can either remove the pinky finger or leave it in place and allow the B and E strings to ring together to create a wonderful ambiguous sounding chord.

Example 6d

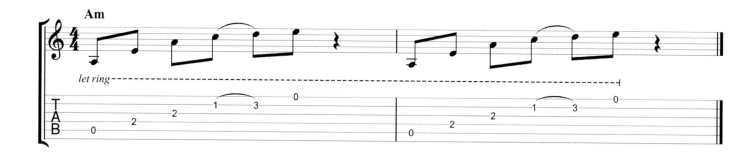

Now let's explore some pull-off patterns. Pulling-off from the second fret to the open D string creates another open sounding chord.

Example 6e

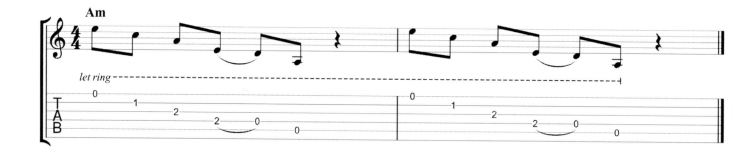

Relocating the pull-off to the G string and executing it with the ring finger turns the standard A minor chord into an Am7 in Example 6f.

Example 6f

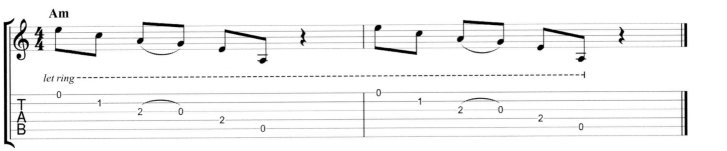

Example 6g has a pull-off on the B string, played with the index finger.

Example 6g

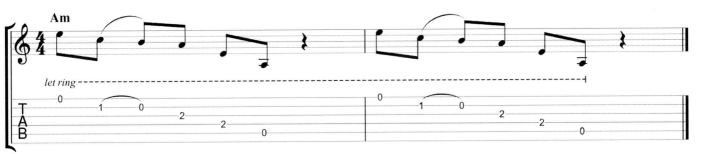

For Example 6h, fret the full A minor chord and pull off from the pinky to first finger on the B string.

Example 6h

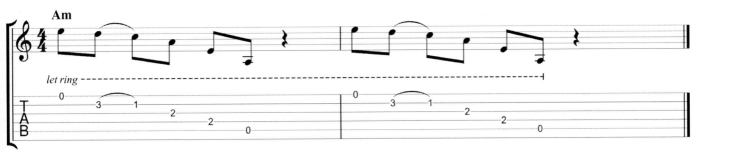

Example 6i combines hammer-ons and pull-offs in a two-bar example and creates a lovely effect when played smoothly. In bar one, you can either hold down the A minor chord to begin with, then lift each finger in turn, or don't hold down the chord at all and add each finger as it's needed. At the beginning of bar two, the full chord will be in place and you can execute the pull-offs normally.

Example 6i

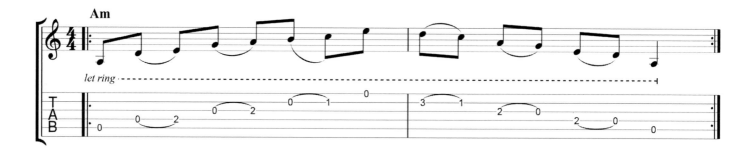

E Minor Legato Patterns

Now let's look at how to add legato embellishments to an open E minor chord. The additional notes will come from the E Natural minor (E, F#, G, A, B, C, D).

The first time I remember hearing how cool hammer-ons and pull-offs can sound was when I heard the track *Oh Well* by Fleetwood Mac. (It uses the E Blues scale but is based around an open E minor chord shape and is one of the most iconic blues-rock riffs of all time).

Our first example adds a hammer-on from the open A string to the second fret, played with the index finger.

Example 6j

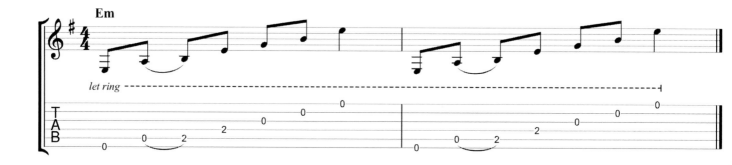

The next common adaption to the E minor chord is to add a hammer-on to the second fret from the open D string.

Example 6k

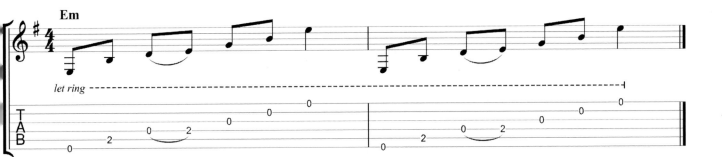

Combining the previous two examples creates an extremely popular legato pattern which is used in pop, rock, blues, country and folk guitar.

Example 6l

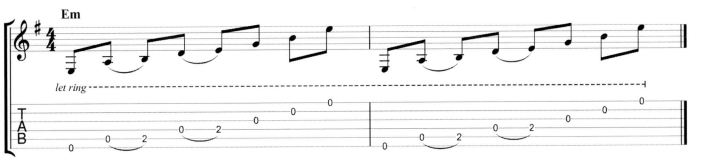

Now we'll reverse these patterns and play them with pull-offs. Pick the chord descending and pull off from the second fret to the open A string.

Example 6m

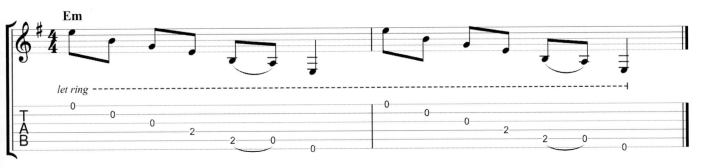

Next, move the pull-off to the D string.

Example 6n

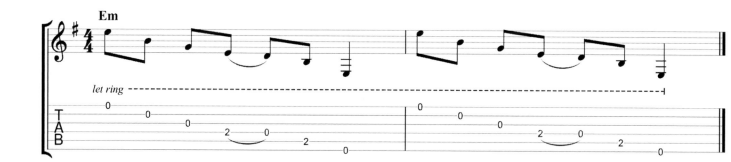

Now add a pull-off on both the D and A strings.

Example 6o

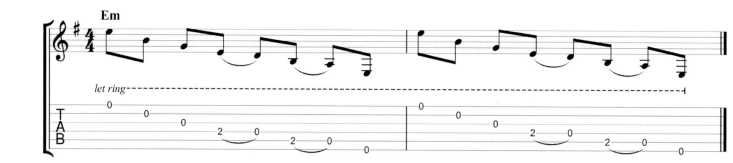

D Minor Legato Patterns

Next we move on to the open D minor chord. The additional notes will come from the D Natural Minor scale (D E F G A Bb C).

Example 6p shows a very common addition to the open D minor shape, with a hammer-on from the open G string to the second fret with the middle finger. You'll hear this sound a lot in folk and country music.

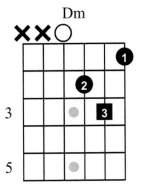

Example 6p

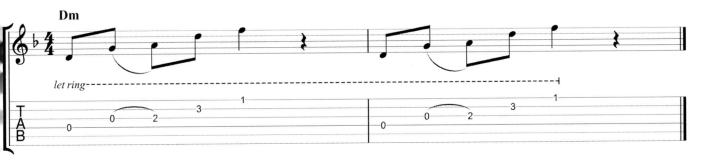

In Example 6q the hammer-on is played on the high E string with the index finger.

Example 6q

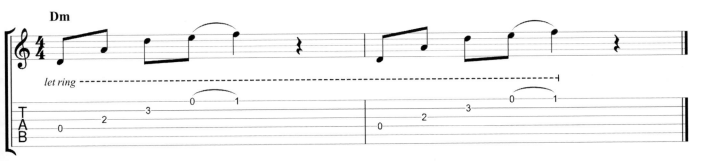

For Example 6r, hold down the D minor chord shape and hammer-on from the first to third fret on the high E string with your pinky finger.

Example 6r

Now let's introduce some pull-off ideas. Playing a pull-off from the second fret to the open G string with the middle finger, allowing the strings to ring out, creates another lovely open sounding chord.

Example 6s

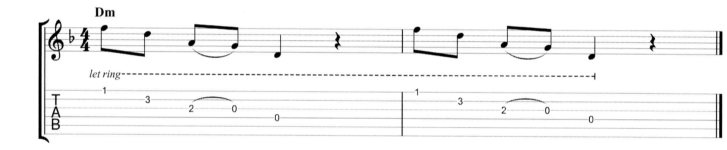

In Example 6t we move the pull-off to the high E string, played with the index finger, before descending through the D minor chord shape.

Example 6t

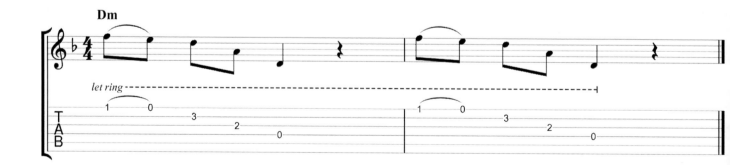

For the final D minor example, fret the full chord shape and pull-off from the third to first fret with your pinky finger.

Example 6u

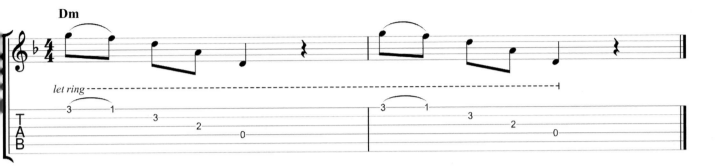

Combining Major and Minor Legato Patterns

In the next examples we'll begin to combine legato patterns to a progression that has both major and minor chords.

A cool way to begin building a legato sequence is to take just one idea and apply it throughout the progression. Example 6v demonstrates this by applying a simple pull-off in the middle of each bar. Play through the example slowly to begin with and work on playing the pull-offs smoothly.

Example 6v

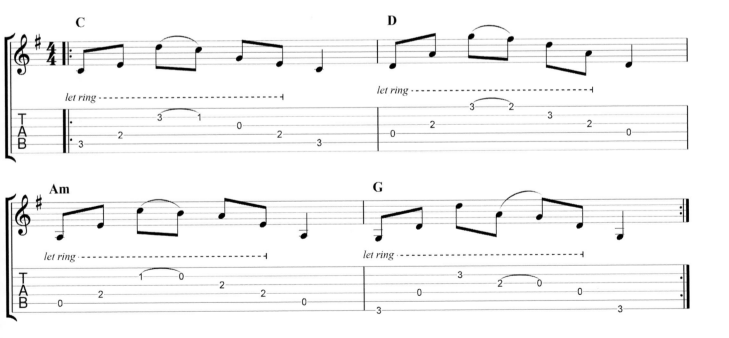

Example 6w uses what is known as a *call and response* phrase. In other words, a pattern that is played and then echoed. In bar one the D minor and C Major chords form the "call" and in the next bar the A minor and E minor chords echo the phrase in response.

Example 6w

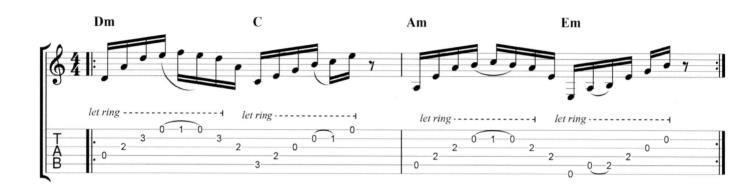

I hope the ideas we've covered in chapters 5 and 6 have given you lots of ideas to push your fingerstyle playing forward. Once you've practiced these examples, get out the chord charts to some of your favourite tunes and see where you can add legato decorations to the chords.

Chapter Seven – Performance Piece: Flood the Light

Everything you've learnt in this book so far has been leading up to a final performance piece that combines as many of the techniques you've learnt as possible. Called *Flood the Light*, it contains a wealth of ideas that you can adapt and absorb into your playing, as well as learning it as a performance piece. I'm confident it will be a piece you'll want to revisit for many years to come.

Flood the Light is written in G Major and centres around chord voicings that use open strings. I have broken down a few of the fills from the track into bite-size examples, so that when you learn the full piece it will feel less daunting.

Before you attempt the examples in this chapter, I recommend listening to the full tune. I've also recorded a performance video of the piece that can be seen at the link below.

www.fundamental-changes.com/beginner-acoustic-videos

Example 7a is a D Major Blues lick (D, E, F, F#, A, B) that repeats a melodic pattern across two octaves. You will notice that the pattern includes legato and slides to accentuate the phrase.

Example 7a – D Major Blues Lick

Example 7b is a "cascading" lick that uses the G Major scale (G, A, B, C, D, E, F#). The cascading effect is created by using a pull-off on one string, then playing an open string on the string below. This pattern repeats through multiple strings and gives the lick a harp-like quality which is a real winner. It's a great idea to add to your fingerstyle acoustic arsenal.

Example 7b – G Major Cascading Idea

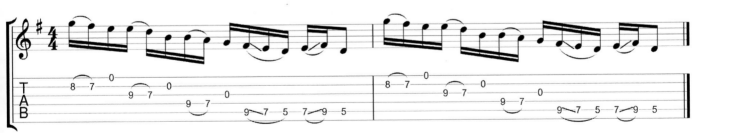

The next part of the piece that is worth practising separately is a Paul McCartney-style run down using the mini-chord patterns we encountered earlier. Here, the mini-chords are arranged on the A and B strings and use the high E string as a reoccurring drone note.

Example 7c – McCartney Style Run Down

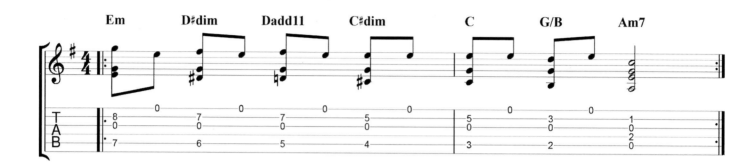

Now that you have practised a few of the more complex elements of the piece, it's time to tackle the full arrangement. Before attempting it, practise the chord shapes that make up the piece.

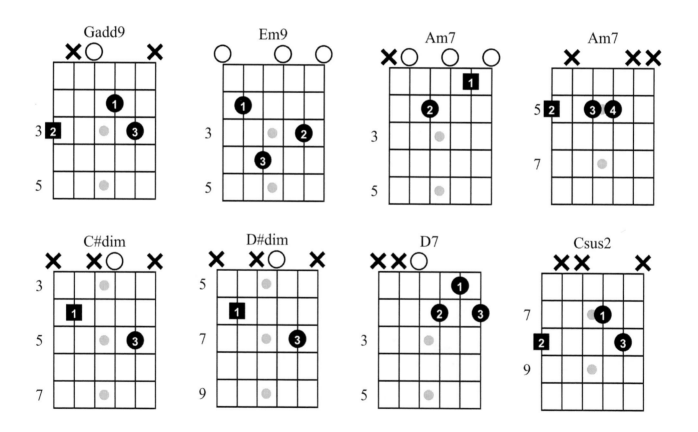

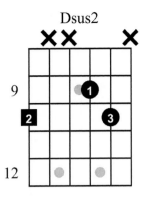
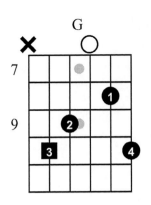

Flood the Light

Example 7d

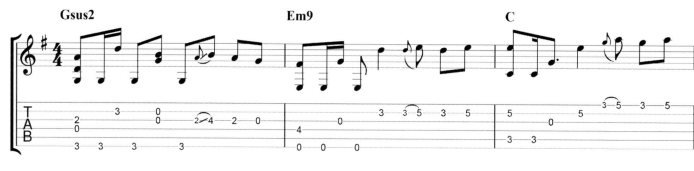

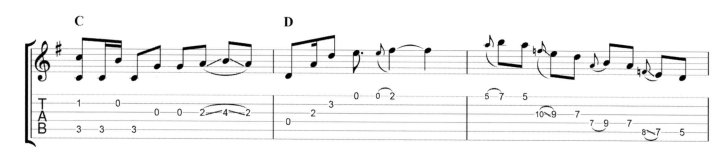

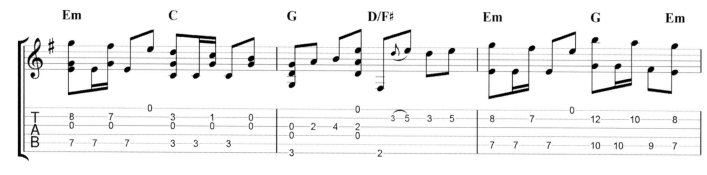

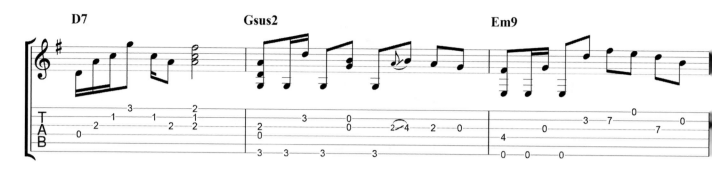

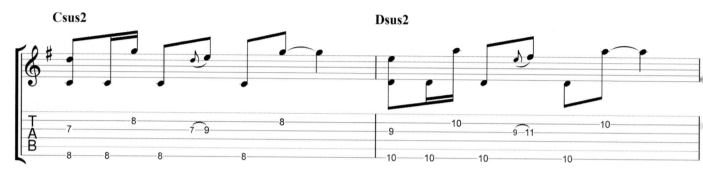

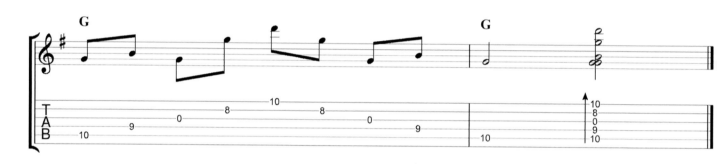

Conclusion

Whether you are just beginning your journey or are an experienced guitarist who wants to perfect their fingerstyle technique, I hope you've benefitted from the ideas in this book. Use the examples as a starting point for creating your own fingerstyle patterns, phrases and complete songs. Let your ears guide you and don't rely on the fingering patterns and scale shapes where you know the "safe" notes are located. My motto is, "If it sounds good, it is. If it sounds bad, it probably is too!"

The best advice I can give to any musician is, *practise what you don't know, not what you do*. We only grow as musicians by pushing boundaries and playing things we've never played before.

An important musical goal should be to play with other people, so while you are developing your skills in this book, find time to jam with other musicians. Playing with other instrumentalists is the best way to improve.

My passion in life is teaching people to play and express themselves through the guitar. If you have any questions, please get in touch and I'll do my best to respond in due course.

You can contact reach me at **simeypratt@gmail.com** or via the contact form at **www.fundamental-changes.com**

Simon.

Made in United States
North Haven, CT
01 October 2023

42221163R00050